CRITICAL ACCLAIM FOR
THE WORKS OF JAMES RADA, JR.

The Last to Fall
"Authors Jim Rada and Richard Fulton have done an outstanding job of researching and chronicling this little-known story of those Marines in 1922, marking it as a significant moment in Marine Corps history."
- *GySgt. Thomas Williams*
Executive Director
U.S. Marine Corps Historical Company

"Original, unique, profusely illustrated throughout, exceptionally well researched, informed, informative, and a bit iconoclastic, "The Last to Fall: The 1922 March, Battles, & Deaths of U.S. Marines at Gettysburg" will prove to be of enormous interest to military buffs and historians."
- *Small Press Bookwatch*

Saving Shallmar
"But Saving Shallmar's Christmas story is a tale of compassion and charity, and the will to help fellow human beings not only survive, but also be ready to spring into action when a new opportunity presents itself. Bittersweet yet heartwarming, Saving Shallmar is a wonderful Christmas season story for readers of all ages and backgrounds, highly recommended."
- *Small Press Bookwatch*

Battlefield Angels
"Rada describes women religious who selflessly performed life-saving work in often miserable conditions and thereby gained the admiration and respect of countless contemporaries.

In so doing, Rada offers an appealing narrative and an entry point into the wealth of sources kept by the sisters."
- *Catholic News Service*

Between Rail and River

"The book is an enjoyable, clean family read, with characters young and old for a broad-based appeal to both teens and adults. Between Rail and River also provides a unique, regional appeal, as it teaches about a particular group of people, ordinary working 'canawlers' in a story that goes beyond the usual coverage of life during the Civil War."
- *Historical Fiction Review*

Canawlers

"A powerful, thoughtful and fascinating historical novel, Canawlers documents author James Rada, Jr. as a writer of considerable and deftly expressed storytelling talent."
- *Midwest Book Review*

"James Rada, of Cumberland, has written a historical novel for high-schoolers and adults, which relates the adventures, hardships and ultimate tragedy of a family of boaters on the C&O Canal. ... The tale moves quickly and should hold the attention of readers looking for an imaginative adventure set on the canal at a critical time in history."
- *Along the Towpath*

October Mourning

"This is a very good, and very easy to read, novel about a famous, yet unknown, bit of 20th Century American history. While reading this book, in your mind, replace all mentions of 'Spanish Flu' with 'bird flu.' Hmmm."
- *Reviewer's Bookwatch*

Continue your adventure in history with three FREE historical novels from James Rada, Jr.

Visit *jamesrada.com/newsletter-email*
and enter your email
to receive your FREE novels.

To Amy,

Who dragged me out to Allegany County
and then had to drag me away from there because I
wound up loving it.

SECRETS OF ALLEGANY COUNTY

Little-Known Stories & Hidden History
From Mountain Maryland

Other books by James Rada, Jr.

Non-Fiction
- Battlefield Angels: The Daughters of Charity Work as Civil War Nurses
- Beyond the Battlefield: Stories from Gettysburg's Rich History
- Clay Soldiers: One Marine's Story of War, Art, & Atomic Energy
- Echoes of War Drums: The Civil War in Mountain Maryland
- The Last to Fall: The 1922 March, Battles & Deaths of U.S. Marines at Gettysburg
- Looking Back: True Stories of Mountain Maryland
- Looking Back II: More True Stories of Mountain Maryland
- No North, No South: The Grand Reunion at the 50th Anniversary of the Battle of Gettysburg
- Saving Shallmar: Christmas Spirit in a Coal Town

Black Fire Trilogy
- Smoldering Betrayal
- Strike the Fuse
- Frostburg Burning

Secrets Series
- Secrets of Catoctin Mountain: Little-Known Stories & Hidden History Along Catoctin Mountain
- Secrets of Garrett County: Little-Known Stories & Hidden History of Maryland's Westernmost County
- Secrets of the C&O Canal: Little-Known Stories & Hidden History Along the Potomac River
- Secrets of the Gettysburg Battlefield: Little-Known Stories & Hidden History from the Gettysburg Battlefield
- Secrets of the Washington County: Little-Known Stories & Hidden History Where Western Maryland Starts

Canawlers Series
- Between Rail and River
- Canawlers
- Lock Ready

Fiction
- October Mourning
- The Rain Man

SECRETS OF ALLEGANY COUNTY

Little-Known Stories & Hidden History
From Mountain Maryland

by
James Rada, Jr.

LEGACY
PUBLISHING
A division of AIM Publishing Group

SECRETS OF ALLEGANY COUNTY: LITTLE-KNOWN STORIES AND HIDDEN HISTORY FROM MOUNTAIN MARYLAND

Published by Legacy Publishing, a division of AIM Publishing Group. Gettysburg, Pennsylvania.
Copyright © 2022 by James Rada, Jr.
All rights reserved.
Printed in the United States of America.
First printing: July 2022.

ISBN 978-1-7352890-5-2

This is a collection primarily of articles that have previously appeared in *Allegany Magazine, Cumberland Times-News,* and *Maryland Life.* In some cases where additional information is available the stories have been updated.

Cover design by Grace Eyler.

315 Oak Lane • Gettysburg, Pennsylvania 17325

CONTENTS

Allegany County, Maryland 1
Life in Allegany County 5
   Allegany County Partied Like It was 1899 7
   A Ride Through the Country 18
   Cumberland's First Phone Call 22
   Allegany County Starts Offering Kindergarten 27
   Allegany County Goes Biking 30
   All They Knew was that 33
      It Filled Their Empty Bellies
   Relic Collection Gives 37
      Picture of Indian Life in the Area
   Start Your Engines! 40
   Allegany County in the War of 1812 45
   When the Celanese Plant 51
      Gave the World a Christmas Gift
Crime & Punishment 57
   Moonshining in the Mountains 59
   Allegany County's First Murder Trial 73
      Started in Washington County
   Flintstone Man Tries to Drive the Pentecostals Out 90
   An Uninvited Guest Terrifies Families 92
   Lover's Triangle Ends in Murder 94
   Tragic Murder Remains Unsolved 100

Canal Life **103**
    The Engineering Marvel Hidden Under a Mountain 105
    The Murders that Didn't Happen on the Canal 111
    Forging Through the Mountains 117
When Coal Was King **121**
    Maryland Government Goes Into the Mines 123
    In Coal Blood 126
    Rats Fleeing a Sinking Ship 134
Odds & Ends **137**
    A New County from Allegany and Garrett 139
    The Last of the Crow Wolves in Cumberland 142
    Frostburg Firemen Answer the Call 146
    The First State-Supported Hospital in Maryland 149
    Luke Gets Connected to Maryland 153
    Get a Taste of Delicious Beef Ham 156
    The Allegany County Auto Industry 159
    The French Sculptor from Lonaconing 163
    Where's General Braddock's Lost Gold? 166
    Crewless Bomber Flies Over Allegany County 171
    County Veteran Who Survived 174
        Andersonville Prison Dies
    How a Small Town Got a State College 177
    A Bridge Over Troubled Waters 191
Acknowledgments **195**
About the Author **197**

Allegany County, Maryland

Allegany County was originally part of Prince George's County when Maryland formed in 1696. As the population in the region grew, new counties broke off from Prince George's County: Frederick County in 1748, Montgomery and Washington counties in 1776, Allegany County in 1789, and Garrett County in 1872.

Before Allegany County was created and its borders established, Virginia claimed parts of the area as Hampshire County, which was created in 1758. County maps of Virginia in the late 1700s show this, and some tax records for Hampshire County can be found in Maryland records and vice versa.

By the time Allegany County was created in 1789, white settlers had established themselves in the area. Thomas Cresap, a frontiersman who was "a hired ruffian, an Indian trader, a land speculator, a farmer, and a soldier," according to the National Park Service, is considered the first white settler in the area. At one point, his home was the furthest point west in the region that the British control. The home site, along the Potomac River, is now near the present-day eastern border of Allegany County. Cresap founded Oldtown in 1741.

Christopher Gist, an agent for the Ohio Company, built a stockade and trading post at the confluence of Wills Creek and the Potomac River in 1749. Gen. Edward Braddock expanded it to become Fort Cumberland in 1755, and this would eventually grow into the county's largest city of Cumberland.

One of many notable figures in Allegany County's history is George Washington. He first came to the area in 1755 as Braddock's aide-de-camp at Fort Cumberland, which was still part of Frederick County at the time. He returned thirty-nine years later as President of the United States, and although the land was the same, it was now Allegany County, and he was in the City of Cumberland.

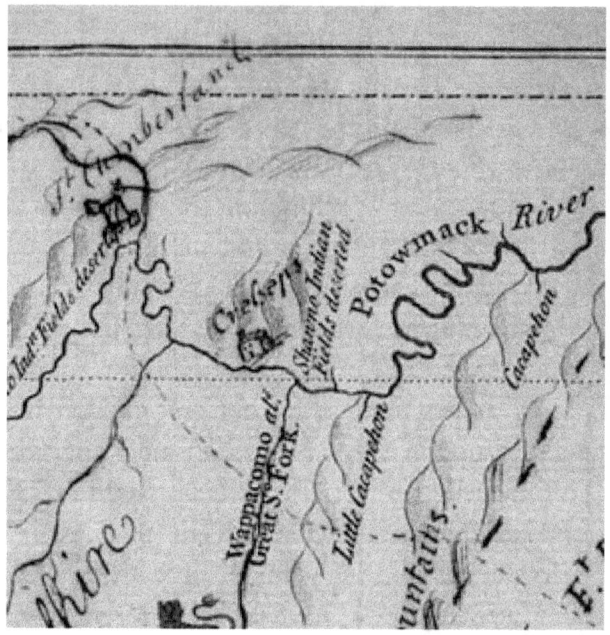

Section of the 1747 Fairfax Map of Western Virginia Showing Cresap's Home. Courtesy of the National Park Service.

Allegany County got its first federal post office in 1795, its first school in 1798, and first courthouse in 1799. All of these were in Cumberland, which became the county's first incorporated municipality in 1815.

The county's rich coal resources helped attract settlers and industry. The county grew as it became easier to travel there. The Baltimore and Ohio Railroad opened in Cumberland in 1842.

As the county grew, towns and cities formed and incorporated: Cumberland (1815), Frostburg (1839), Westernport (1859), Lonaconing (1890), Barton (1900), Midland (1900), and Luke 1922.

Garrett County was formed from the western end of Allegany County in 1872, making it the last county created in Maryland.

Allegany County thrived in the late 1800s and early 1900s. It reached its largest population of 89,556 in the 1950 U.S. Census. Since then, the population has declined each decade as industry has left the county, with a few exceptions. In the 2020 Census, the county population was 68,106.

It remains a popular destination for people who enjoy history or the outdoors.

The Allegany County Seal.

Life in Allegany County

Allegany County Partied Like It Was 1899

In 1789, Washington County gave birth to Allegany County. It had some settlements in it at the time, but by and large, the area that would become Allegany County was a frontier. The preamble of the act from the Maryland General Assembly that created Allegany County read:

"Whereas, A number of the inhabitants of Washington county, by their petition to the General Assembly, have prayed that an act may pass for a division of said county by Sideling Hill Creek, and for erecting a new one out of the Western part thereof; and it appearing to this General Assembly that the erecting such a new county will conduce greatly to the due administration of justice, and the speedy settling and improving the western part thereof, and the ease and convenience of the inhabitants thereof..."

The area might have been a frontier, though, but year after year, it grew as people moved westward in search of land and opportunity.

When the county turned 100 years old in 1889, the residents decided to celebrate their centennial with a three-day celebration.

The *Cumberland Times* previewed the celebration reporting, "This will be a grand affair-one which will not only be a pleasant reunion of friends of former years and of relatives, but one which will result in some benefit to the county generally, and bring the name and resources of Allegany more prominently before the country at large. Our city will be gay with rich bunting streamers, flags and other decorations. Every one is anticipating a good time and Cumberland will do its best to make it a joyful and pleasant occasion for all visitors. Come and help us celebrate our 100th birthday!"

The centennial medal from Allegany County's centennial celebration. Courtesy of Whilbr.org.

The Centennial Celebration

Cumberland residents were encouraged to decorate their homes, particularly those homes along the grand parade route, so that the city would look decked out for a party. "It is hoped that every family and place of business throughout the town, whether on the line of parade or not, will put up flags, bunting and other decorations to brighten up our city, so that strangers and visitors may see what Cumberland can do when all take an interest. Let every one do something towards decorating, and our city will present a fine appearance," one advertisement read.

The Georges Creek Railroad planned to run excursion trains between Lonaconing and Cumberland to bring people into the city for a reduced fare. The Cumberland and Pennsylvania Railroad did the same thing for county residents in the Westernport area. People outside the county could purchase special fares on the Baltimore and Ohio Railroad and the Pittsburgh and Connellsville Railroad to visit Cumberland for the party.

Despite rain, a hot-air balloon was filled and ascended 1,000 feet into the air. Professor Foust jumped from the basket wearing a parachute and floated to the ground. Courtesy of Whilbr.org.

The celebration was spread over three days—September 23-25, 1889—in Cumberland.

The first day featured a massive parade of school children

from around Allegany County. Just about every school sent a group to represent their school. The divisions featured: 1) special guests and the day's speakers, 2) private schools and schools outside of Cumberland, 3) Cumberland schools and 4) "colored" schools. The parade route was about three-quarters of a mile long and ran from Union Street to the county courthouse.

The military and civic parade through Cumberland during the centennial celebration. From the Herman and Stacia Miller Collection courtesy of the Mayor and City Council of Cumberland.

The second day of the celebration had a parade of county tradesmen and a daring leap from a hot-air balloon. "Prof. J W Foust, of Lewisburg, Pa, was the aeronaut, and sat on the trapeze until hundreds of yards high in the air, when he jumped to the ground supported by a parachute, alighting along the Baltimore and Ohio road near the weigh scales, about five hundred yards from the Queen City hotel. The balloon proper turned over in the air, the hot air escaped and it descended some distance further on. Prof. Foust was heartily congratulated by the thousands of spectators on the success of his feat. The balloon was in the air about five minutes," *Cumberland Times* reported.

According to most reports, the balloon reached around 5,000 feet, but the professor jumped with his parachute around 1,000 feet.

Rain fell on the second day of the celebration, though most activities continued. The fireworks display and boat parade had to be postponed to the final day.

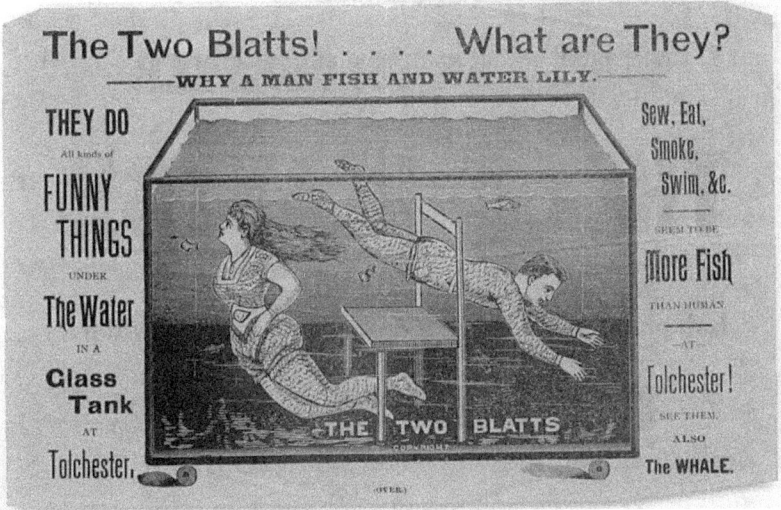

The Blatts offered to perform during the centennial celebration, although it is uncertain whether the entertainment committee selected them. The back side of the handbill reads: Exhibition in a large glass tank, full of water. Their record is 4 1/2 minutes under Water. Really a sight worth seeing! Go see the whale! Courtesy of Whilbr.org.

The newspaper described the boat parade on the final day. "The boat parade on the Potomac, under the management of A H Dowden, took place about 8 o'clock. The steamer Endeavor started up the stream from near the dam with the Electric Cornet Band on board playing familiar airs that were exceedingly pleasant to the ear as the strains were wafted over the waters. When reaching Lynn's wharf the boats were swung into line and then formed four and five abreast with lanterns swaying to and fro, the reflected light in the waters beneath continuing an uninterrupted circle of brilliancy and oscillating illumination that was attractive to the eye and pleasing in its novelty. Down stream the boats glided, the movement in keeping with the time of the music, and as the night was dark as Erebus, the contrast made a picture that seemed ideal rather than realistic, and placed the parade in the memory of the visiting populace as one of the features of the Centennial celebration."

The parade featured that day, though, was a military and civic parade led by U.S. President Benjamin Harrison. The newspaper headline described the parade as "An Unbroken Column in Soldierly Attire, Secret Orders in Beautiful Regalia, Bands, Fire Companies, Floats, and Carriages." The reporter then went on to note, "it occurred to many that the presence of the President of the United States upon this historic spot was a fitting link to bind the events of a little over a hundred years ago, when George Washington, the first President of the United States, stood upon the same ground, then almost a barren waste, to the new century of the county's existence about to begin."

Saving Memories

Following the celebration, Col. Theodore Luman, who was the vice chairman of the Centennial Celebration General

The handbill advertising the parachute leap from a hot-air balloon. Courtesy of Whilbr.org.

Management Committee, collected souvenirs, artifacts, ribbons, the Centennial edition of the *Cumberland Times*, medals and photos in a box. "The box will then be hermetically sealed and placed in the vaults of the Court House, there to rest until 1989," according to the newspaper report.

Sometime during the next century, the box must have been moved from the courthouse. It wasn't opened in 1989, nor was its disappearance even noticed.

The staff of the Allegany County Public Library found the box in 2002 as preparations were being made for renovations to the main library branch building. No one had ever seen it before that time, but it had Luman's name on it and a special piece of the county's history inside of it.

Come Home

This poem was printed on the back of the letter inviting people to Allegany County's Centennial Celebration. The Centennial Bulletin noted, "it is from the pen of a well-known lady of this city."

> How many years? a hundred,
> Since she into being came
> And musical Allegany
> Was given her for a name!
> And now, to her sons and daughters
> North, South, and East and West,
> How far so ever you wander
> Away from the home-land nest,
> Wherever the wide world holds you
> Under the heaven's blue dome,
> She sends to you all the summons
> To her birthday fete — come home.

Secrets of Allegany County

Was she your Cinderella
O sister counties proud?
She hath envied not your riches
Nor Shame her head hath bowed.
Oh, fair are your sunny gardens
That lie on the Eastern shore,
And charmed are your wooded inlets
That the wild duck wingeth o'er;
Oh, yours are the crab and oyster
Down by the shining bay,
And the wealth of orchard-acres,
Rosy with bloom in May.

Come, when the sumac reddens,
Glimm'ring bright in the sun;
When the summer''s heats are waning
And the summers toil is done;
When the harvests home are gathered
And the happy fields are calm;
When the mountains' robes are gayest,
And the mountain air is balm.
What memories must draw you,
Of by-gone hopes and fears,
To learn what the brave old county
Can show for a hundred years!

But old Allegany's laurels—
She hath won and worn them well.
And the history of her triumphs
Her gifted sons shall tell.
And still shall our own Potomac
Winding down to the sea,
Witness a greater glory

JAMES RADA, JR.

In the days that are yet to be.
Here waits the dear old mother
The absent ones to greet;
Then, "whatever skies above" you,
Hither ward turn your feet.

Come, if the world has used you
Well, since the far-off time
Of your free and careless boyhood,
When you learned these hills to climb;
Come, if a fate unkinder
Has followed wher'er you roam;
Who knows but a brighter fortune
May await you here — come home.

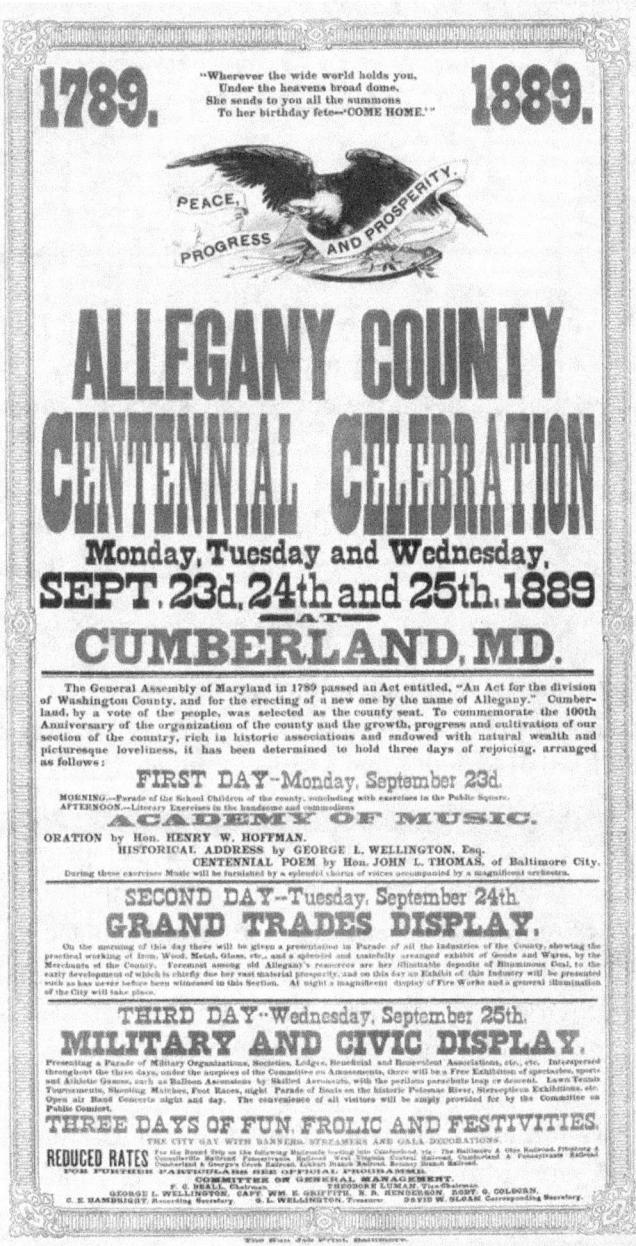

A hand bill announcing the centennial celebration. Courtesy of Whilbr.org.

A Ride Through the Country

On a lovely June day in 1856, ten men left Baltimore on the Baltimore and Ohio Railroad to travel its length and see the country. A special train consisting of an engine, dining car, two cars with reading rooms and writing rooms, and a passenger car carried them on comfort along their journey. One of the men, Brantz Mayer, wrote about the trip and *Harper's Weekly* published it in April 1857.

The iconic *Harper's Weekly* began in 1857 as "a journal of civilization." It became famous for its coverage of the Civil War and sketches of the events. This early version ceased publication 1916, although several revivals have been attempted over the years.

Mayer noted that it was only recently that people could enjoy their trips into the mountains. "It has only been of late that bolder minds have ventured to restore romance to travel by scaling the Alleghanies with steam-engines, and making a jaunt through our upland dells and forests as great a delight as it was to those who first penetrated our wilderness," he wrote.

It was raining when the group reached Cumberland at around 4 p.m. Mayer wrote, we "were soon relieved from anxiety as to accommodations by our generous friends in this charming city. We should do violence to their feelings if we spoke publicly of what is habitual with them and characteristic of the country; but we should equally violate ours if we avoided the expression of gratitude for a pleasant season in Cumberland, spent in the midst of unostentatious people and 'old Maryland hospitality.'"

A drawing of the Cresap House in the mid-1800s from *Harper's Weekly*.

The following morning, the group boarded a special train owned by the Eckhart Mining Company to get a tour of the county's coal region. Mayer described the Narrows as a "splendid gap, which extends for more than a mile, five hundred feet wide, with precipitous walls of near nine hundred!"

Mayer wrote that the Eckhart Mining Company must be one of the prosperous businesses in the district "owning a railway, several villages, ten thousand acres of coal land, immense quantities of timber and farming country, and employing about six hundred workmen."

Mayer had been in a coal mine previously, so he did not take the tour of the mine with the other men in the group. Instead, he sat on the hillside admiring the panorama view.

They then took a carriage ride further up the mountain

and saw "a vestige of Braddock's Road, which the patriotic owner has fenced in, for fifteen or twenty yards, as a post-and-rail monument to the defeated General?"

They also passed through Frostburg "a fresh mountain village, flourishing under the impetus of an increasing neighborhood."

A drawing of Eckhart Mines in the mid-1800s from *Harper's Weekly*.

Then it was on to Mount Savage with its mix of industry and "cultivated society."

They finally returned to Eckhart and rode the Eckhart Mines train back to Cumberland.

"I know few inland towns more charmingly situated than Cumberland, on the slope of a superb amphitheatre, with its background of mountains, approached through vistas of forest-covered spurs," Mayer wrote.

He noted that most trace of the old historic Fort Cumberland had vanished and were replaced with new growth. They did walk the hill where the fort had been located walking around a "Gothic Church, which occupies the site of the fort, and 'whose *canons*' as a joker said, 'have displaced the *cannons* of the fort.'" He noted that a depression in the ground marked the site of the old well that had served the fort.

On Greene Street, the group was shown two houses that were supposedly built by General Braddock. They were made of heavy timbers with iron bands and rivets on the side. Although they were homes in 1856, originally they were supposed to have been a jail and a court.

Late in the day, the group boarded the B&O Special and headed south, skirting along the Potomac River to New Creek in Virginia (modern-day Keyser, W.Va.). Their journey would eventually take them west to the Ohio River.

A drawing of the Narrows outside of Cumberland from the mid-1800s from *Harper's Weekly*.

Cumberland's First Phone Call

A 1976 article in *The Cumberland News* reported that telephone service in Allegany County began in November 1880. However, articles in *The Daily Alleganian and Times* place the beginning of telephone usage in the county years earlier, shortly after Alexander Graham Bell uttered, "Mr. Watson, come here. I want to see you."

An article in the newspaper on Valentine's Day 1878 noted that the Consolidation Coal Company had the first telephones in Cumberland "which promises to become so valuable," the newspaper noted.

In those days, telephone wire was run between two telephones, providing a direct connection between those two phones and only those two phones. So, although the Consolidated Coal Company had the first telephone in Allegany County, it's not as if calls could be placed all over the world or even all over the city. The first regular telephone line had only been established the previous year between Boston and Somerville, Mass. The first telephone company would not even be established until later in 1978.

The Consolidation Coal Company line ran from the office on Centre Street to the telegraph office and from there to the freight depot of the Baltimore and Ohio Railroad. The total distance was a little over half a mile.

The way it worked was when the telegraph office received messages for either the coal company or the freight depot, a call could be placed from the telegraph office to either location. The same worked in reverse if either location needed to send a telegram. However, if someone in the coal office needed to talk to someone in the freight depot, C. H. Walker, the telegraph operator, had to relay the message between two telephones.

The Daily Alleganian and Times praised the telephone, saying that "a conversation can be readily carried on between two parties, so plainly that the voice of the speaker can be recognized. Last evening songs were sung at each end of the line by Messrs. Brenneman and Steiner, and the notes were clearer and more distinct than when in the presence of the singer."

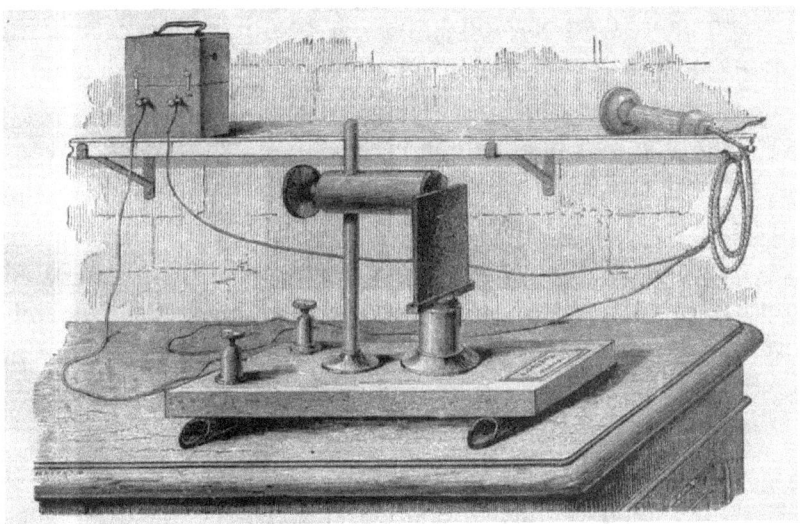

The Edison Carbon Telephone, one of the early telephone designs.

With the telephone's success, plans were made to run a phone line from the Cumberland to Mount Savage and from there to Frostburg.

The one problem that the newspaper noted was that the telegraph and telephone lines were on the same poles. This proximity allowed anyone listening on the telephone to hear the dots and dashes of telegraphic communication so clearly that the listener could interpret the Morse Code message.

"We were such annoyed yesterday by the clacking of the instrument in the Western Union office, although it was not within 50 feet of the telephone wire," the newspaper reported.

The following month, the newspaper noted that a new telephone was being tested in town to try to avoid the problem of line interference. Two Phelps Hand Telephones were placed in the Western Union Telegraph Office.

"A large number of persons have examined the instruments and tried them to their entire satisfaction. Persons speaking in Cumberland could be heard distinctly, and in many instances voices could be recognized and the name of the speaker called," the newspaper reported.

The Phelps Hand Telephone was one of the many inventions and advances that William Phelps contributed to the field.

"During his long and productive career, Phelps invented and improved printing telegraph systems, set design standards for many telegraph instruments, invented stock tickers and telephone instruments, and built the patent models for some of Edison's early inventions," according to the website Telegraph-History.org.

Other than private telephone subscribers, the first telephone service in the county was established in November 1880, and the first central office where people could go to make telephone calls was in the Mountaineer Fire Engine House on South Liberty Street.

The Chesapeake and Ohio Canal started using the telephone along the canal in 1879 when a single violinist played his music near Hancock for an audience in Cumberland.

"The telephone on the canal is quite a novel thing as well as a great convenience to the employees," the Cumberland *Daily Times* reported in 1879. "The sound of a violin was heard distinctly in the collector's office last night, which was played at the locks 50 miles distant from this city.

This short concert marked the completion of wiring the old transportation route with the latest communications technology — the telephone.

The C&O Canal Company had originally wanted to run a telegraph line along the canal and started erecting poles to carry the wires. A survey was made of the canal in 1878 "for the purpose of constructing a Telegraph line and establishing stations at proper points for the transaction of the company's business and to expedite the making of repairs when necessary," according to a report to the canal president and board of directors.

However, the officers realized that each telegraph terminal they installed would need to be staffed by a skilled operator. They realized it would be far cheaper, at least in terms of labor costs, to install telephone lines instead of telegraph lines because any canal employee could use the telephone.

The idea was to string the telephone wire on existing telegraph poles that the superintendents of the different divisions on the canal were currently using for communication. With that expense minimized, the cost was expected to be only $14,000. However, upon final inspection, it was discovered that the existing poles were too light for the load that would be required, and new poles would need to be installed. Some areas also needed to be cleared of overhanging trees that could interfere with the telephone lines. According to the report to the canal company, the new poles "would not only carry wires to provide for the addition of other wires from time to time as the wants of the company might require."

Construction began on March 12, 1879, and the telephones were put into operation as each new section of wire was strung. The complete line from Georgetown to Cumberland went into operation on October 1.

Each mile of canal route had 30 chestnut poles erected to a height of 25 feet. Each pole, which was at least six inches in diameter, had to be buried five feet in the ground. The line was powered by 10 gravity batteries on the ends and five batteries at each telephone. Communication was done through 48 "Edison Universal telephones."

Although the installation of a phone system along the canal was a large expense, the canal company believed it would see other savings to offset the installation and maintenance of the phones.

"The simple and easy method of communication by telephone adapts it peculiarly well to canal transportation service, and the facilities afforded to work and transportation on the canal must and will very soon dispense with a number of superintendents and other employees necessary under the present management," according to the report to the canal company.

When the project was complete, it used 5,665 poles; 69,300 pounds of wire; 7,500 screw glass insulators; and 6,000 brackets. It was also one of the longest phone lines in the country at the time.

A century after Alexander Graham Bell's first phone call, the telephone had become such a large part of American life that the Allegany County Commissioners recognized "Telephone Centennial Day" on March 16, 1976.

Allegany County Starts Offering Kindergarten

Schools had already started in the fall of 1970 when enrollment in Allegany County Public Schools suddenly jumped by nearly 8 percent. Schools around the county welcomed 1,247 kindergarten students for the first time 12 days after other students returned to the classroom.

The *Cumberland Evening Times* reported that Allegany County was one of the last counties in Maryland to offer kindergarten. During the 1969-1970 school year, only Allegany, Carroll, Charles, Cecil, Frederick, and Talbot counties did not offer kindergarten. However, the Maryland General Assembly passed legislation requiring school systems to offer kindergarten, although students were not required to attend.

Kindergarten is a German invention that encouraged play to help children develop. A kindergarten day started with songs and then allowed children to play with different toys that allowed them to learn and explore the world around them. The first kindergartens opened in the United States in 1856 in Wisconsin. The idea slowly spread from there.

Given the Maryland requirement to offer kindergarten in 1970 and Allegany County's delayed start, the county might have been the last county in Maryland to offer kindergarten.

With the decision made for the county to offer kindergarten, it fell to the board of education to decide how to implement it. It was decided to "phase" it in by delaying the start, so brand new kindergarten students and teachers wouldn't be caught up in the hustle and bustle of the first days of school. This would allow any kinks in how the program operated to get worked out without the distractions of problems that typically occur on the first day.

The board also decided to pattern its curriculum after Howard County's curriculum, although Allegany County would develop its own "after we get a year under belt," according to Wayne Hill, the secretary-treasurer of the board.

The board also voted not to accept kindergarten students from out of state, at least for the first year, although out-of-state students were still allowed for grades 1-12.

Training for 20 teacher's aides who would help with the kindergarten classes began in June at the Allegany Community College Early Childhood Development Center.

The board planned to have 24 kindergarten classrooms in the county, with half of them in the old Allegany Community College building on Frederick Street, which was named the Kindergarten Center. Alma G. Logsdon, the former Lavale Elementary principal who served three years in the army during World War II, was named the principal of the center.

The need for classroom space was minimized because the kindergarten program was only a half-day program with morning and afternoon groups of students.

On Sept. 18, 1,247 five-year-olds showed up for class. This brought total enrollment in the school system up to 17,704 students, an increase from 16,448 students the previous year. Nearly half of the new students (611) were in the Kindergarten Center. Besides the Kindergarten Center, the other elementary schools with classes were Central School in Lonaconing, Cresaptown, Flintstone, Frost, Hill Street, Mt. Savage, Oldtown Fire Hall, Thomas G. Pullen, Luke Community Center (former Luke School).

The program cost was $350,000 (about $2.4 million in today's dollars) and was expected to increase the county's tax rate by 13 cents to $2.61.

Allegany County Goes Biking

On a beautiful, sunny July day in 1897, hundreds of Allegany County residents visited the Tri-State Fairground and paid a quarter each to watch professional racers. The spectators weren't coming to see auto racing or horse racing. They wanted to see bicyclists.

"The track has been specially dragged, scraped, and rolled, and will be smooth as cement pavement," the *Evening Times* reported.

The turnout was phenomenal, considering the races had been announced two days prior.

The first true bicycle (called a velocipede) raced along the streets of Paris in the early 1860s, and mass production began in 1868. It spread to the United States that same year.

This early bicycle was uncomfortable to ride, in part, because they used wooden wheels banded with iron. This earned the velocipede the nickname of "boneshaker" because the rider felt every bump down to his bones.

The idea remained popular, and people worked to improve the ride. The "safety bicycle" came along in the 1890s. It had two wheels of equal size, a chain-drive transmission, gear ratios, and inflatable tires. This version proved to be a hit and created the bicycle craze in the United States.

It was not a cheap hobby, though. The average cost of a bicycle was $75 (about $2,000 today). People bought them despite the fact that the country was in an economic depression.

The first known bicycle race in the country was in Boston in 1878. Cumberland began hosting amateur races in 1892. They were usually shoehorned in between horse races and foot races as the fairground.

Bicyclists during the bike riding craze of the late 1800s.

Cumberland's amateur races were dominated by one man. "In 1892, in order to promote the bicycle races in Allegany county, the Times offered a handsome gold medal for the best amateur rider in the county. Mr. Archie C. Wilson won the medal that year and has held it ever since as his personal property," the *Evening Times* reported.

The opportunity arose to host a professional bicycle race in the county in 1897, so a series of races were put together including a one-mile novice race, a half-mile race for African-Americans, a half-mile boys' race, a one-mile amateur championship race, a half-mile amateur race, and a one-mile professional race. Some of the races had three heats, but others were a single race.

A special prize of $10 (about $500 in today's dollars) was offered to the fastest rider in any race if he could ride a mile in under 2:10 (nearly 28 mph). If this seems fast, a professional cyclist, Charles M. Murphy, rode on a wooden track behind a Long Island Rail Road train two years later and rode a mile in 57.8 seconds, which earned him the nickname Mile-a-Minute Murphy. No one won the Allegany County's special prize, but more than $200 in prizes (about $10,000 today) were awarded to the winners of the various races.

The race judges were Judge John T. Edwards, Douglas LeFevre, and Taylor Morrison.

Wilson donated his gold medal to be melted into a gold bar that would be inscribed with the names of the winners.

Lee Deale was the overall winner of the professional race.

All the racers were males. This was because many women didn't ride because it was cumbersome to do so in long dresses, which were common attire for women of the day. Some women who did want to ride wore blousy trousers called bloomers and were often ridiculed for it.

The bicycle craze soon peaked, and interest fell off. Nationwide sales of bicycles fell 79 percent from 1897 to 1904, according to the U.S. Department of Commerce.

All They Knew was that It Filled Their Empty Bellies

Elementary school students at Hammond Street Elementary in Westernport filed through the lunch line receiving plates of hot roast beef, mashed potatoes, and green beans. They didn't realize they were also receiving service from a premier food service operation. They only knew it was a warm lunch that filled their sometimes-empty bellies.

"Qualified school authorities and nutrition experts have stated in recent months that the lunch system adopted in Allegany County schools is second to none in the country and in fact is far superior to similar systems in schools throughout Ohio, Pennsylvania, West Virginia and a number of other states," The *Cumberland News* reported in September 1945.

The reason for the praise is that most schools at the time had no cafeteria operation. Children instead brought their lunches to school in a lunch box. When there were cafeteria staff to serve lunches, it was generally a cafeteria director who cooked and prepared the food, assisted by older students who served lunches to students in large city schools.

Allegany County changed that concept, not only for the county but for the country.

In August 1944, the board of education requested a part-time nutritionist from the Cumberland and Allegheny Gas Company. Nutritionist Flora Dowler was sent to assist the board and W. P. Cooper, the food program director for the board, who was already a pioneer in school food service.

Dowler's work began with two days of training for the cooks at Fort Hill High School, where she demonstrated and prepared different types of lunches that met state guidelines and could be prepared on premise. She followed that up with similar visits to each school at least once a month.

Students at East Side Elementary line up for school lunches in the 1940s. Serving lunch in elementary school was a unique concept pioneered by the Allegany County Food Service Association beginning in 1939. The glass milk bottles on the tables were recycled for repeated use. Cardboard milk cartons were introduced in the 1950s. Courtesy of the Allegany County Food Service Association.

During those visits, she discovered a lunch program that had been started in 1939 in Hammond Street Elementary School.

The board, working with the Works Progress Administration, the Surplus Marketing Corp., Maryland Department of Public Welfare and the school's Parent Teacher Association provided free lunches to 60 percent of the students at the school.

Dowler said this was needed because "most of the bus children attending this school came from the region where the coal mines were practically abandoned and the parents unemployed."

The program's success led to its expansion to all other schools in the county.

"This beginning has resulted in offering hot lunches daily to three-quarters of the school children in the county," said Dowler.

The program was able to operate on a county-wide basis because of support from the War Food Administration and the Maryland Department of Public Health. The War Food Administration provided financial support and food. The Maryland Department of Public Health examined the 76 cafeteria employees and inspected the lunch rooms to make sure they were sanitary.

At the time, cafeterias weren't available in every school. Four schools served their students lunch in the auditorium, and students at Corriganville Elementary ate lunch in their classrooms.

Columbia Street School was the only school where there wasn't a lunch program, and that was because there was no space for a cafeteria. However, by 1945, work was under way to remedy this problem.

Once the program was expanded county wide, 26 schools served 8,400 type A lunches daily, 14 schools served 3,300 type C milk lunches daily, and 20 percent of the county's 15,000 students were receiving free or reduced-price lunches.

The cost of a school lunch was 60 cents a week or 15 cents daily. More than two million lunches were served in Allegany County schools during the 1944-1945 school year.

"Although no scientific research has been conducted to prove the value of this program, teachers, county nurses and principals feel the need for it and are most gratified with the results of the program to date. Some tests have been made in various schools and results indicate better health, better school attendance and improved scholarship," said Dowler.

For her work in pioneering the new cafeteria system, Dowler received the annual McCall Magazine award for outstanding work in her field.

Relic Collection Gives Picture of Indian Life in the Area

They were just pieces of wood that Jesse Valentine found while digging in the ground, but to him, they meant so much more. As he dug around the wooden posts that were set in a circle, he realized that he had the floor of an Indian teepee, which soon led to the uncovering of an entire village.

He carefully examined each shovelful of red loam that he removed from the earth. Soon, he was finding a variety of artifacts. A clay pipe that was decorated with straight and zig-zag lines. A dozen leaf-shaped flint dishes. They were "found buried twelve inches below the surface in a circle, each one overlapping the other," the *Cumberland Evening Times* reported. "They were placed there by some ancient flint maker and forgotten. They were intended for making arrows or spear heaves at some future time." Though found in other Indian excavation sites, these were the first found in Western Maryland, according to Valentine.

He also found mussel shells, turtle shells, and deer horns, giving some indication of what the long-dead Indians had eaten.

The Shawnee had occupied the village from around 1680 to 1700. They had migrated from South Carolina and camped along the Potomac River in locations that ranged from Keyser to Oldtown.

"Eventually, white settlers forced them to migrate west to join other Shawnee tribes in Ohio," the newspaper reported.

Jesse Valentine with his relic collection. Scanned from the *Cumberland Evening Times*.

The camp that Valentine excavated was the largest Indian camp site in Western Maryland and part of the reason for his life-long obsession with artifact hunting. However, it was only a hobby for Valentine. He was a brickyard operator and farmer by trade.

Valentine's father, Frank, had started the artifact collection on June 7, 1889. That is when he started hunting for artifacts. He logged each relic with the date and place where he found it. The collection grew over the years into thousands of pieces.

Because he sought artifacts all of his life, Frank started

taking his son along with him on his hunts. By the 1950s, Jesse had also caught the artifact hunting bug and was doing it on his own. When his father died, their artifact collections numbered in the thousands.

"Many of the rare finds were made on the James Pollack farm which is located in Maryland across the Potomac River from the Miltenberger farm," the *Cumberland Times* reported.

According to Valentine, a person could stand on Knobley Mountain and look down on the camp and see a dark circle created by stones laid out around the camp.

"There is a burial ground located near this camp, which local Indian authorities say was the location of a tribe of prehistoric Indians," the *Cumberland Times* reported.

Valentine had found three skulls in the burial ground, one with a flint arrowhead embedded in it, which indicated that the person had been murdered. The skeleton of Indians baby was also found in the burial ground.

He started displaying 3,000 relics in a small museum. The skulls were part of the collection, as were pipe bowls drilled in curved rocks. "The drilling flint was chipped in the shape of a T, strapped on a shaft and twirled in the hands to cut the hole," the newspaper reported.

Similar tiny drills were found that helped drill bone beads. There were also mortars and pestles, including one that was 2.5 feet long. It was hung from a branch and dropped into the large mortar. It made grinding and mulching easy.

The Valentines had so many items of certain types that they traded items with relic collectors in the Midwest. So their collection came to include gouges, adzes, axes, and spades that had been used by the Mound Builders.

They continued to display the collection for years to educate the public on how some of the first settlers in the area had lived.

Start Your Engines!

The Cumberland Municipal Airport has never been busier than when sports cars raced around its runways.

Yes, sports cars. Not airplanes.

Each May from 1953 to 1971, racers from across the country would travel to Cumberland to test their sports cars against other top cars to see whose was the fastest. Roger Penske, Shelby Briggs and Carroll Shelby all raced at the Cumberland Airport. The races featured some of the greatest racing cars of the time: Birdcage Maserati, Ferrari Testa Rossa, D Type Jaguar, Porsche 356 Speedster, Cobra, Mustang, Camaro, Sunbeam Alpine, Austin Healy 100, and the Howmet Turbine Car.

"It was a great time," said Dave Williams. "A who's who of American sports car racing came through Cumberland." Williams watched many of those old races as a young man and he remains a racing enthusiast and promoter of sports car racing today.

The Cumberland Municipal Airport offered a 1.6-mile-long course for the racers. In the days before permanent automobile racetracks became common, airport runways offered a satisfactory alternative.

Cumberland Lions Club staged the annual races and their proceeds helped provide free eye exams and glasses for needy children in the county, helped build Lions Manor Nursing Home, contributed to the Wilmer Eye Clinic at

Johns Hopkins and funded the local Salvation Army, Boy Scouts of America, and YMCA.

May 1953 saw the first races at the airport. It resulted from months of planning between officials from the airport, Cumberland Lions, and Pittsburgh Steel Cities Region–Sports Car Club of America.

The program from the 1957 races at the Cumberland Municipal Airport.

"The initial 1953 event started as Steel Cities/Pittsburgh Regional Races with 80 entries and a rather sparse group of spectators," Bob Poling and Bill Armstrong wrote in *Wings over Cumberland: An Aviation History.*

Word spread locally and through the racing community that the airport in Cumberland was a great track on which to race.

The following year, 122 racers and their cars showed up to compete before a crowd of around 12,000 people. This led to Cumberland's regional event becoming a national one.

"Being a national event meant that it was the most-important event in your region in a year," said Williams.

It also meant that only racers with a national competition license could compete at Cumberland. There were only 1,100 nationally licensed drivers in the country at that time, and 284 of them showed up in Cumberland to race in 1955. They came from 40 of the 48 states, Washington, D.C. and Canada. The racers competed in 11 races from 8:30 a.m. until 4:15 p.m. giving racing fans a full days of thrills.

Spectators gather at a high vantage point to watch the races at the airport.

As a national event, Cumberland began getting featured in media across the country. *Sports Illustrated* listed the Cumberland Airport Races among the big coming events in the world of sports.

"It represented the largest car race conducted in the US and included many prominent racing figures such as the

Briggs Cunningham team of Maseratti race cars. Also, the American manufactured Corvette was making its presence known," wrote Poling and Armstrong.

The Cumberland Sports Car races continued to grow in popularity with fans. Some highlights over the years include:

- 1956–Band leaders Paul Whiteman and Skitch Henderson along with actor Steve Allen race in Cumberland.
- 1957–Famed racer Carroll Shelby wins the main event at Cumberland.
- 1958 - Roger Penske taking his SCCA driver's test in Cumberland in a 283 Corvette. Penske got his license at the cost of his car. He blew the engine and then it fell off the trailer as he took it home.
- 1965–The new GT Mustang driven by Bob Johnson wins the Production Car race.
- 1966–The Walt Hansgen Memorial Trophy is awarded in memory of a five-time winner at Cumberland. Hansgen was killed in a crash at LeMans earlier in the year.
- 1967–What would become a classic—the Z28 Camaro—won its first race.
- 1968–Ray Heppenstal drove the turbine-powered Howmet TX Turbo car. Billed as the "car of the future", it lost its race to Bob Nagel's McKee Ford 427.

The peak year for the races, as far as attendance goes, was 45,000 people in 1958. This was also the year a racer went over the embankment at the airport. Louis Jeffries was driving a Siata Special when the brakes failed coming off a long straightaway. The car went over the embankment, rolling several times until it reached the bottom. Jeffries was injured, but not seriously. It was the only time that this type of accident happened during the races.

"By the early 1960s, though, airport courses were being

replaced by permanent sports tracks and attendance at airport races declined," said Williams.

Though the community supported the races, some people were complaining about the ground at the airport being torn up and that the cars racing at Cumberland were starting to show their age.

Then the Cumberland Mayor and City Council voted to ban car races at the airport after June 1971. This allowed the 1971 race to go on. Only 200 cars entered the races and competed against each other before 12,000 fans. Almost as if to mark the sadness of the last airport races in Cumberland, it rained through much of the day.

The Federal Aviation Administration agreed with the actions of the city government. In a letter to the city, an FAA official wrote that "it is evident that increased use of the airport requires that all facilities be available for aviation purposes."

Amateur racing had been struggling in recent years not only because access to airports was being denied to organizers, but insurance costs for such events were rising dramatically. Also, many of the big-name draws for these events had turned professional, taking much of the fan base with them.

Allegany County continues to have autocrosses, but nothing like the head-to-head competition that once thrilled residents.

Allegany County in the War of 1812

Some historians call the War of 1812 the second American Revolution. Less than a generation after America won her independence, she once again found herself battling Great Britain. It was a war that neither side wanted because both countries were still trying to recover from the original American Revolution.

The British fought a defensive war in the early years of the War of 1812 because they were also fighting against Napoleon Bonaparte and the French army and navy in Europe. By 1814, the British had beaten Napoleon, and they turned their attention more fully to ending the war with the United States with a victory. Up to this point, most of the fighting had been around the Canadian and U.S. border. In the Mid-Atlantic, the British had started a blockade in 1813.

"During the years of Madison's administration, from March 1809 to June 1812, the English continued their insults, aggressions, and depredations. Our harbors were insulted and outraged, our commerce swept from the ocean, our seamen impressed into British fleets, scourged and slaughtered, fighting the battles of those who held them in bondage, and studied indignities were offered to our national flag wherever displayed. All efforts for redress from the British government had failed, and at length (acting in accord with a majority of the Senate and House of Representatives of the United States) the President issued his proclamation declaring war against Great Britain on the 18th day of June 1812," J. Thomas Scharf wrote in *History of Western Maryland*.

Preparing for War

In July 1814, President James Madison called on the states to supply militia to defend the young country. According to William Lowdermilk in *A History of Cumberland, Maryland*, "Maryland was required to furnish one Major-General, three Brigadier Generals; one Deputy Quartermaster-General, one Assistant Adjutant-General, and six regiments, to consist of 600 artillerists, and 5,400 infantry."

However, war is a political question as well as a military one, and Maryland was split on the need to go to war. The Federalists called themselves the "Friends of Peace." Their position was that the U.S. should fight only to defend its borders and not seek to take territory from Canada, which had been happening on the northern front of the war. The Democrats were called "War Hawks" and fully supported not only a defensive war but an offensive one.

In the fall elections of 1814, the Democrats nominated Thomas Cresap, Thomas Greenwell, Benjamin Tomlinson and Upton Bruce to the state legislature. It was the Federalists who swept the election, though. Jesse Tomlinson, William McMahon, William Hilleary and Jacob Lantz were elected and sent to Annapolis to represent the county.

Around that time, the county also moved towards filling its portion of the state's militia quota and there was "a considerable degree of enthusiasm manifested," according to Lowdermilk.

While county residents hadn't been engaged in any military conflicts since the Revolutionary War, volunteer groups had been meeting to drill, shoot targets and discuss fighting techniques. Lowdermilk wrote that some of the volunteers had served in the Revolutionary War as members of the Maryland Line.

Maryland soldiers had distinguished themselves for their bravery and ability during the Revolutionary War. They were so dependable that it is said George Washington called the Maryland regiments his "Old Line," which is where one of Maryland's nicknames as "The Old Line State" comes from, according to the Maryland Archives.

Troops fighting during the War of 1812. Courtesy of Wikimedia Commons.

Answering the Call

In the fall of 1814, two companies were formed in Allegany County that totaled 227 fighting men. Captain Thomas Blair formed one company primarily with men from Cumberland. Captain William McLaughlin formed his company with men outside of the city.

Lowdermilk noted of Blair's company, "The Company formed in Cumberland was made up of excellent material, the organization having been effected some months before."

Once formed, the men marched to Baltimore in August where they became part of the First Regiment of Maryland Militia, under General Samuel Smith and Colonel John Ragan. They spend most of their time at Camp Diehl wondering if they would see any fighting.

Seeing Action

On September 12, a British fleet of more than 30 warships and transports sailed up the Chesapeake Bay and landed 5,000 troops on the North Point peninsula. The American militia of 3,000 men, including the soldiers from Allegany County, met the British troops at Godly Wood, eight miles north of the British landing point.

The two sides exchanged musket and artillery fire for about an hour before the British troops' superior size forced the Americans back toward Baltimore. However, the Americans inflicted heavy casualties on the British, including mortally wounding the British commander Maj. General Robert Ross.

With the loss of the lionized Major-General Robert Ross to tree-hidden American sharpshooters, the British advance toward the city slowed whilst the powerful fleet lay useless against Fort McHenry because of the tremendous amount of blockage which had been dropped into the channel," according to the General Society of the War of 1812 web site.

The bombardment of Fort McHenry, which led to Francis Scott Key to write the words to "The Star-Spangled Banner," began the following day.

As a side note, Key's original poem, "The Defence of M'Henry," was originally published in nearby Hagerstown in the *National Songster of 1814*, according to the *Hagerstown Town and County Almanack*, which also owned the publication.

The almanac's website notes, "is that though it appeared in many songsters, the VERY FIRST appearance of the poem as a song under the title, 'Defence of Fort M'Henry', was in 'The National Songster', Hagerstown, Maryland in 1814 with the direction that it be sung to the tune of To Anacreon of Heaven. This publication was the product of John Gruber, founder of The Hagerstown Town and Country Almanack! This has been corroborated by many bibliographies of American Songsters from 1734 to 1820."

The Battle of North Point as painted by Thomas Ruckle. Washington County soldiers distinguished themselves during the battle. Photo courtesy of Wikimedia Commons.

Celebrating

Back in Allegany County, news reached the residents of the American victory on Lake Champlain between New York, Vermont and Quebec and the people celebrated. "Processions paraded the streets, singing and shouting, and the entire population took part in the celebration," Lowdermilk wrote.

The county's soldiers were mustered out on October 13, after which they returned to the county and were disbanded in early November.

When the Celanese Plant Gave the World a Christmas Gift

On Christmas Day 1924, the American Cellulose and Chemical Manufacturing Company gave the world a gift that continues to this day. It came with little fanfare, probably because the plant had seen so many delays in opening that "t seemed the gods themselves had declared war on the Cumberland plant," Harry Stegmaier, Jr. wrote in *Allegany County–History*.

However, the Dreyfus Brothers had pushed forward, mounting roadblock after roadblock, to create an artificial silk from cellulose acetate fiber that would be free from the drawbacks of silk.

Doctors Camille and Henri Dreyfus began pursuing their dream in the early 1900s as they conducted chemical experiments in a shed in their father's garden in Switzerland. By 1910, the brothers had developed cellulose acetate lacquers and plastic film. This success led to a commercial product that allowed the brothers to fund further experiments. They built a manufacturing plant and made a nonflammable motion picture film base that eventually replaced the volatile cellulose nitrate base, according to the Celanese Corporation website.

The Dreyfus brothers continued experimenting and by 1913 they had created a high-quality acetate fiber yarn.

World War I took their research in a new direction, and they produced a flame-resistant acetate lacquer coat (called acetate dope) for fabric used to cover airplane wings and fuselages. The brothers also moved their operations to Britain from Switzerland where they believed they would be safer. The new company was called the British Cellulose and Chemical Manufacturing Company, Ltd.

With the U.S. entrance into WWI, negotiations began to bring the British Cellulose and Chemical Manufacturing Company to America. The potential location for an American plant required that it be far enough away from the coast to avoid possible Zeppelin attacks, near a plentiful source of water, and near the cotton belt, since cotton was the primary cellulose source the company used.

"Cumberland's location suited the company's requirements. Moreover, it possessed good rail transportation and lay near a source of cheap fuel," Stegmaier wrote.

The Cumberland Development Company bought three farms and parts of three others to create the plant site.

"In 1918, after a year of negotiations and delays, Cellulose & Chemical Manufacturing Company, Ltd. was opened in Cumberland, Maryland, to produce acetate dope for the U.S. military," according to the Celanese Corporation website.

Before plant construction could be completed, though, the war ended, and the demand for the acetate lacquer nearly disappeared. Work continued on the plant, but at a snail's pace because of construction and labor issues.

Meanwhile, operations in the England plant resumed, and in 1921, the Dreyfus brothers produced the first cellulose acetate yarn. Not only did it not have the problems silk had, it was far less expensive. Cellulose acetate yarn sold for $9 a pound as opposed to $20 a pound for silk. Cellulose acetate yarn had its own production problems that needed to be worked out. The initial yarns couldn't be manufactured with a consistent diameter. The biggest problem was the textile industry didn't know how to use the yarn, in part, because the traditional dying process to create fabric colors didn't work on cellulose acetate yarn. The company set to work developing new machinery, processes, and dyes to address the problems.

The American Cellulose and Chemical Manufacturing Company began manufacturing cellulose yarn on Christmas Day 1924. Courtesy of Whilbr.org.

This early form of artificial silk was used from primarily for crocheting, trimming, and effect threads, and for popularly priced linings, according to the Celanese website.

In 1922, when the company decided to trademark its new product in England, it offered a 5-pound prize for a name. Celanese, which was said to be a combination of "cellulose" and "ease", won.

By 1923, the company had $13 million dollars in orders. Then a textile depression hit, and all the orders were cancelled, which threw the company into financial problems. Work on the Cumberland plant continued with portions opening, but then the spring of 1924 saw two floods devastate the region. The spinning and textile buildings at the plant were damaged. Materials washed away in the flood waters and machinery was covered in mud.

This caused increased financial difficulties for the company, and Cumberland officials began worrying the deal would fall apart and the company wouldn't open its Cumberland plant. The race to start production started and on Christmas Day, the company began weaving a refined cellulose acetate yarn that addressed many of its problems. While the event revolutionized the textile industry and saved the company, it only merited a small article on the *Cumberland Evening Times* business page, which noted "It is said that the demand for the silk is far greater than the supply and that the market for it will be widespread."

This new yarn was an instant hit, so much so, that the silk industry tried its best to discourage companies from using it. Users realized the Celanese had good wrinkle recovery, good draping, and was quick drying. It had multiple retail uses in things like rugs, bathing suits, and clothing. The only problem was that other companies didn't have the machinery needed to weave the new yarn. To continue the growth of the product, the company started weaving the yarns into fabrics in 1926.

"The remarkable rise in the use of Celanese yarns by the mills in this country has been responsible for one of the most interesting chapters in fabric development that has been noted in the textile markets since the development of synthetic fibers," the trade journal *Textile Bulletin* reported.

The Cumberland plant, which had 550 employees in 1924, soon grew to have 7,000 employees in Cumberland 10 years later. During World War II, demand for Celanese skyrocketed because the material made here in Allegany County was used in military parachutes.

The success of Celanese was so great that in 1927, the American Cellulose and Chemical Manufacturing Company became the Celanese Corporation.

Celanese continued to win over customers. According to the Celanese website, "At the time acetate was introduced in the U.S. practically all better dresses were made of silk; by the 1950's less than two percent were silk." The Celanese was one of the dominant sellers in the market at the time.

As new synthetic fibers and competitors entered the market, Celanese began looking to diversify its product offerings. This initially helped the company's sales grow, but by the late 1960s, many of its operations for these new products were sold off when foreign markets slowed. As the company grew and expanded into other countries and states, operations began shifting. By the time the Cumberland plant closed in 1983, only 310 employees remained. The plant was eventually razed and the state prison built on the former site.

The Celanese Corporation still exists today, although not in Cumberland. It is based in Texas with a number of foreign offices and employs around 7,500 people worldwide – the same number of people it once employed in Allegany County alone at its peak. The company has also diversified its offering in various areas, including engineered materials, acetate tow, chemistry, food ingredients, and polymers.

CRIME & PUNISHMENT

Moonshining in the Mountains

When the sale, production and transportation of alcohol were banned in the United States in 1920, Western Marylanders had to choose between becoming teetotalers or criminals. Many law-abiding citizens chose the latter.

"Illicit liquor, manufactured in countless stills in homes, farmyard barns, and even auto repair shops, could be bought all over the county." Harry Stegmaier, Jr. wrote in *Allegany County–A History*.

One of the first raids in the county on these places where illegal liquor was sold and produced came about almost accidentally. On June 2, 1920, Elmer Dumar, owner of the Vimy Restaurant on North Mechanic Street, was not very happy. His wife, Jennie, had spent part of the evening flirting with "a Spaniard," according to the *Cumberland Evening Times*. Dumar finally lost his patience and got into a fight with the Spaniard. The man ran off and called the police.

"The Vimy Restaurant had long been a source of trouble for the local police and it was suspected that whiskey was either being sold outright in one of the rooms adjoining the restaurant, or else being made somewhere on the premises. The police chief decided once and for all that the local police department would get the inside story of the numerous fights that had kept them busy running to the Vimy during the past year," Herman Miller wrote in *Cumberland Through the*

Eyes of Herman J. Miller.

The police raided the restaurant and the Dumar apartment above it. They found two moonshine stills, six barrels of corn mash, four gallons of moonshine, and other equipment for producing liquor. The Dumars and three other men were arrested.

Revenue agents display their captured moonshine. Courtesy of the Library of Congress.

The first arrest in Frostburg of someone violating the Volstead Act, the name of the legislation enacting Prohibition, didn't happen until October 21, 1922, nearly three years after Prohibition started. By then, the city had a statewide reputation for out-of-control drunkenness and not enforcing Prohibition.

A 1921 front-page article in the *Cumberland Evening Times* proclaimed: "Vice Crusade on Town Evils in Frostburg. County Bootleggers and Prostitutes Have Made It Headquarters in Recent Weeks."

"Certain near-beer saloons sell moonshine openly over the bar, while 'etherized' beer that carries a kick and sickening after-effect, is dispensed by the truckload by the county 'rum ring,' assisted by Pittsburg bootleggers," the newspaper reported.

Many of the bars also had "ladies parlors" and winerooms where the prostitutes seem to have met up with their johns. The *Cumberland Evening Times* reported that during the Declaration Day celebration, it was estimated 100 prostitutes came to Frostburg from Keyser, Cumberland, and the towns along the creek. They attended a dance in the backroom of a saloon in Frostburg, where they plied their trade.

The newspaper also reported that "cocaine artists" from Cumberland came to the city to hold "snow parties."

Unpopular law

Though Prohibition was not popular nationwide, Maryland was nearly defiant in its attitude toward the law. Maryland was the only state not to pass an enforcement act, and it still called itself a "wet", not "dry", state.

A *Cumberland Evening Times* editorial proclaimed in 1920, "On the bootlegging proposition the police commissioner is probably right in his conclusion that the United States army would not be able to stop drunkenness entirely. This probably would be true so long us preventing drunkenness depends upon the enforcement of so extreme and unreasonable a measure as the Volstead act which, in its entirety is not respected by one reasonable person in ten."

The mayor of Lonaconing, John H. Evans, must have agreed with the sentiment. He was arrested for moonshining in 1942.

However, no matter how unpopular Prohibition was, law enforcement officials did their jobs. According to Miller, so many arrests were made for bootlegging and illegal liquor sales during Prohibition that the Allegany County Jail couldn't hold everyone at times, and the excess prisoners had to be kept in the Garrett County Jail in Oakland.

Police show captured confiscated moonshine after the car hauling it crashed. Photo courtesy of the Library of Congress.

George Hawkins

One of the reasons for so many arrests in Allegany County was due to the work of federal agent William R. Harvey. He could be considered Allegany County's Eliot Ness.

"He could not be bribed, and he achieved quite a local reputation for his persistence in tracking down illicit whiskey. At one point, he trailed a bootlegger through the snow for several miles, from the swamp where the man confiscated a cache of moonshine," Stegmaier wrote.

He became such a thorn in the sides of bootleggers that they backed his campaign for Allegany County Sheriff in 1926 because they thought it would give him additional work to do besides coming after them. Harvey won the election and served as sheriff for a time, but he eventually returned to working for the federal government.

If Harvey was Allegany County's Eliot Ness, then Harry Klosterman of LaVale was probably the county's Al Capone. Klosterman was the "king of local bootleggers," according to Stegmaier.

"This amazing gentleman had stills scattered all over the area, including one in a house on Washington Street in Cumberland, right under the nose of the chief federal agent in the area, who lived nearby," Stegmaier wrote.

Despite the comparisons, Western Maryland actually had very little problem with organized crime, such as what was seen in Chicago during Prohibition. The reason for this is that nearly all the moonshine in Mountain Maryland was made locally, so organized crime never had much of an opportunity to get its foot in the door here.

Only a few days after Frostburg's first arrest under the Volstead Act in 1922, citizens were "shocked" when George Hawkins led raids on multiple locations on October 24, 1922. Hawkins and five other police and agents arrested over three dozen men and women in raids on the cellar of the Biddington home, Federal Hill, Hotel Gunter, and St. Cloud Hotel. The raids began at Federal Hill at 7 a.m.

"Throughout the day, Hawkins and his staff hauled the prisoners and loot in one by one," the *Cumberland Evening Times* reported.

Agents seized four stills in the raid and dumped 400 gallons of liquor. According to the newspaper, the jugs, kegs, stills, gauges and other equipment seized in the raids filled one end of the town hall.

"At five o'clock last evening the lock-up resembled a convention hall of a bootlegger's conference," the newspaper reported.

The raid resulted from Secret Service agents visiting the city weeks before in an undercover capacity. They collected information about bootleggers and speakeasies in Frostburg, which they passed on to Hawkins.

The speakeasy that was hidden in the basement of the Hotel Gunter in Frostburg. From the author's collection.

Poole's Garage

On the night of January 23, 1923, Hawkins led a raid on Poole's Garage at 361 Frederick Street in Cumberland.

"The raid, according to Agent Hawkins, resulted in the

capture of one of the largest stills in this section and perhaps the largest in the state," Miller wrote. "Agent Hawkins destroyed the $8,000 miniature distillery found on the third floor rear of the garage building. In addition to three forty-five gallon copper stills, which were in operation when the officers entered the place, they found six 500 gallon steel vats containing about 2,300 gallons of corn mash in the first stage of fermentation, three 50 gallon barrels of 126 proof liquor, six new empty-barrels, hundreds of empty bottles, jugs and jars, and all the conveniences of an up-to-date bootleg factory. In all, there were about 295 gallons of finished liquor in the room, ready for delivery."

It took an hour to destroy the illegal liquor and dismantle the stills. Agents took samples of each barrel and then poured kerosene into the barrels. B.A. Poole, the garage owner's son, was then called in to witness that each vat of corn mash had been poisoned with bichloride of mercury.

Hiding the stills

Because manufacturing liquor was illegal, the stills needed to be hidden out of sight of law-enforcement officials.

"In the Georges Creek region, abandoned mines proved convenient for housing stills and storing moonshine," Stegmaier wrote.

One still was found in a hidden room in a house on Roberts Streets when an oil stove exploded in the room on July 11, 1925. The room was in the cellar of James R. Smith's house. The explosion caught the house on fire, but when firemen arrived, they could see smoke coming through the parlor floor and through the floor around the flue in a front bedroom on the second floor, but they couldn't find the source.

"Finally, against the strenuous protest of the family, they

began to dig through the floors of the parlor and the bedroom. Beneath the parlor floor they found a layer of earth about a foot thick and then a rough board ceiling, which covered a secret room in the cellar," Miller wrote.

The flue from up to the second floor was four-feet wide, but from the second floor up to the roof, it was only 18 inches wide. A ladder in the wide flue led down to the secret room.

Another bootlegger who lived on North Mechanic Street had a platform constructed outside of a second-story window so that it hung over Wills Creek. It was designed so that if the house was raided, the bootlegger need only pull a rope and the bottom on the platform would drop and anything on the platform would crash into the rocks of Wills Creek, destroying any evidence.

Another Cumberland bootlegger wore an overcoat wherever he went.

"People who didn't know him thought he was an eccentric, but he had a half dozen pockets inside the coat in which he carried his stock of whiskey for sale," Miller wrote.

Bars, which were called "speakeasies" during Prohibition, also had to be hidden out of sight. Some of Cumberland's speakeasies could be found on Harrison Street near the American Legion, on Cumberland Street between Baltimore and Market streets, and in many restaurants in the city.

Frostburg gone wild

It appears that little enforcement happened in Frostburg, particularly since it took nearly three years to make a moonshining arrest.

Constable John Lewis arrested Joseph Cavey of Ormand Street for selling moonshine to two brothers named Huston on October 21, 1922. Cavey was released on a $1,000 bond the next day and promptly became the city's second arrest for a Volstead Act violation when he apprehended for selling a pint of moonshine to Elmer Lancaster.

Lancaster had come to Frostburg from Eckhart and "indulged to (sic) freely, resulting in the usual drunken stupor," according to the *Cumberland Evening Times*.

On his way home, Lancaster was thrown from his wagon along Midlothian Road. He apparently then wandered away from the wagon along the road until he collapsed. A passerby found him bleeding from a head wound.

The wound wasn't serious, but when Officer Jabez Mealing arrived, he could smell the liquor on Lancaster. Mealing bandaged Lancaster's wound and took the man to jail. When Lancaster woke up, he told the police that Cavey had sold him the moonshine.

While the National Road was a great benefit to Frostburg in bringing people to the city, it also made it possible for the troublemakers to get to the city easier. Besides loud and drunken people on the streets at all hours of the night, men were often drugged and robbed.

"It is asserted in Frostburg that drunken, sodden men lay around these resorts all day and night and the better element are incensed at conditions," according to the *Cumberland Evening Times*.

The mayor and city councilmen started a clean-up campaign "to arrest all disorderly men and women". They were enforcing new town ordinance on public conduct and not the Volstead Act, which they said they had no authority to enforce.

Although many Frostburg residents were upset with all the disruptions from drunk men and women, they were often making their own wine in their homes. The newspaper noted in 1922 that "many once-Prohibitionists Are Said to Have Been Stung by the Bug." If affected both men and women with the newspaper noting that women "seem more anxious than the men to get the 'proper taste.'"

It was estimated 60 percent of Frostburg families were making wine illegally. "In other words 850 families will have wine cellars or closets this year with approximately 6,000 gallons on hands (unless someone else gets a key to the cellar)," the *Cumberland Evening Times* reported.

The bar in the speakeasy that was hidden in the basement of the Hotel Gunter in Frostburg. From the author's collection.

Water Shortage

In late August 1922, Frostburg residents were facing a water shortage, although there was plenty to drink. The problem was that what was available to drink was moonshine because the moonshiners were using all the water.

As water levels started falling in the town's water system during the summer, officials started investigating to find the reasons behind it. The answer "was finally revealed by discovery in a most unusual way. Just how would be telling a secret," the *Cumberland Evening Times* reported.

Water was being consumed at three times the normal rate. Frostburg typically used about 110,000 gallons of water daily, but it was using 330,000 gallons in 1922.

The reason was the estimated 100 stills operating within town boundaries. The newspaper did the math, estimating that each still used an average of 90 gallons of water an hour or nearly 2,000 gallons to make a batch of moonshine.

The 90 gallon estimate was an average between the 75 gallons an hour used by a small still and the 100 to 125 gallons an hour used by large stills. The average still was using the same amount of water as 20 families.

"One hundred stills will use nearly 200,000 gallons of water, or the exact amount in excess of water supply estimated by an expert from Baltimore, which should be used by a town the size of Frostburg," the newspaper reported.

To deal with the water shortage, town officials circulated flyers listing 12 points urging conservation measures. The flyer was signed by Mayor Olin R. Rice, Josiah Ford, Edwin Elias, Griffith Hughes, Ed J. Duffy, Leslie Hockman and Harry Fuller.

Most of the points were things that would still be relevant today, such as "Do not let water run continuously when washing dishes." "Have a plumber or some competent person to stop all leaks of every kind and also reduce the quantity used in flushing commodes." A few were specific to the time period, such as "Do not let water run to cool milk and butter–buy ice."

The flyer also urged residents to report their neighbors who were breaking the rules to city officials, although they weren't enforcing the Volstead Act. City officials also tried to scare residents, writing, "Our safety and even our existence as a town may depend upon the observance of these rules."

The final point was just for moonshiners. "Mr. Moonshiners, please stop making moonshine until there is more water."

It was never noted whether the moonshiners reduced their consumption of water. Police finally started making arrests a few weeks later, which may have slowed production of moonshine somewhat.

A captured still is put on display. Photo courtesy of the Library of Congress.

The end of prohibition

Due to its unpopularity, Prohibition soon ended after the election of Franklin D. Roosevelt in 1932. However, Allegany County lagged a bit behind the rest of the state in switching over to selling alcohol. A bill passed in the state legislature stipulated that county beer permits didn't become effective until seven days after the sale of beer became legal, which happened on April 7, 1933.

"You could buy beer on the first day of repeal in Pennsylvania. A store just over the state line on the Bedford Road was selling beer on the first day. A steady stream of Cumberlanders took advantage of the beer sale," Miller wrote.

On April 14, beer sales finally became legal in the county and the speakeasies came out in the open to handle the steady business that now came their way.

Moonshining made easy

Besides making moonshine (illegal liquor), bootleggers were also known to make "home brew", illegal beer, during Prohibition. Garrett County miner, Kenny Bray, wrote about some of the recipes in his unpublished memoirs.

Home brew

Ingredients: 1 can malt 0.75, 5 lb. sugar, 1 yeast cake 0.05, 5 gal. water.

Dissolve the sugar and malt in warm water. Add yeast and cover with cloth. "When it begins to ferment, a foam will form on top," Bray wrote. The foam will eventually diminish.

"To tell when it is done, you hold a lighted match down next to the surface of the liquid. If the match goes out, it is not ready. If the match continues to burn, it is ready to bottle," according to Bray.

Moonshine

Ingredients: 1 bushel corn or grain, 50 lb. sugar, 2 yeast cakes, 35-50 gal. water

Moonshine was made in stills. The two major parts of a still were the boiler and the cooling tube. Half-inch copper tubing was run from the boiler (where it was sealed with flour paste to keep an airtight seal) to the cooling tube where it coiled as it ran through the cooling tub until it reached the bottom of the tub.

The ingredients are mixed to make corn mash, which is heated in the boiler. Some bootleggers might add honey to the ingredients and let it ferment with the water and yeast. The resulting alcohol from this was called "Honey Brandy."

"When you were no longer getting alcohol from the worm, you would catch about a teaspoon from it, throw it on the fire. If it flashed, you kept cooking. If it sizzled, you stopped," Bray wrote.

The finished alcohol could be aged in charcoal to give it an amber color or vanilla extract might be added to give it an aged appearance.

The quality of the finished product was determined by shaking the bottle. The shaking caused a "bead" or chain of bubbles to form around the edge of the bottle at the top of the liquid. The longer the alcohol held the bead, the better it was considered.

Allegany County's First Murder Trial Started in Washington County

During Allegany County's first 40 years, people died, and sometimes people killed other people, but 1829 was the first time the county executed someone, and it wasn't even a resident of the county.

George Swearingen was born in Berryville, Va., in 1800. He showed promise at a young age, and by all rights, should have lived a successful, long life. He came from a well-off family and received a good education. He was only 17 years old when he got a job in the office of the clerk of courts in Washington County.

However, George was forced to resign after 15 months due to an illness, but he turned that setback into a positive. He used his time off to study law, and when he got better, he earned his law license.

He eventually returned to Hagerstown to clerk for his uncle, John V. Swearingen, who had been elected county sheriff. George developed a reputation as an amiable and respectable young man.

"I was addicted to the common vices of young men of my age and circle—I was scarcely ever heard to swear—was strictly temperate—never seen out of temper, and rather avoided those places of carnal pleasure and vice which are the sure and certain road of death," George wrote in 1829.

In 1823, James Scott of Cumberland took his daughter, Mary, to Hagerstown so she could attend school there. She boarded with John Swearingen, who was related to her, and George was a cousin "two or three times removed," according to the *Hagerstown Morning Herald*.

Some reports say George was engaged to be married, but his family urged him to break it off to pursue Mary Scott. George wrote he had broken off his engagement a year before, and he made the choice to court Mary.

A letter that was published in multiple newspapers after George's death was purportedly written by someone who spoke with George in his last hours. This person wrote, George said, "I never wanted to marry Mary, but my uncles forced me to marry her. I wished to marry Miss ---- of Boonsborough. Although both of them, personally, though more of Miss ---- yet they preferred Mary because her father was rich."

Mary was young, and George was charming. It did not take him long to win her over. The two were married on February 24, 1824, but it was not a marriage borne out of love.

"Her prospects being flattering, but not more so than my own, I concluded that by uniting our persons and our interests we would have a fair start for wealth, influence and happiness in this world," George wrote.

The couple continued to live with John Swearingen until 1825, when George could afford to build them a home.

"For awhile Swearingen's habits continued to be regular, and if he was not a truly loving husband, he was at least a kind one. He lived with her in peace, neither contradicting, denying her anything, nor setting bounds to her expenses. But, as she was a thoughtless, heedless woman, as might be expected from her age, and was constantly desiring to visit her relations in Cumberland, their harmony was ere long interrupted. It became apparent to his neighbors and friends, that he would gladly have been rid of her," according to the 1836 book *United States Criminal History*.

George was a young man with a bright future. The *Baltimore Sun* said, "George Swearingen was one of the brightest, wealthiest and most popular young men of Washington county. His manner and person were pleasing: he had an obliging disposition and was master of all the arts of obtaining public regard."

That was one side of George's personality. The other side was not so upright and law abiding.

The sheriff was caught in the woman's web

George Swearingen was a rising star in Washington County politics in 1827. He came from a good family, married well, and been elected the county sheriff. He had an Achilles' heel, though, and when it began unravelling his life, it did so quickly.

George's wife, Mary, gave birth to their first child, a girl, in November 1825, while Mary was at her family's home in Cumberland. Her ill health after the birth wound up keeping her at the house for six months.

This frustrated George. His wife's frequent visits to Cumberland and the time it forced George to take off from his work was a point of contention in their marriage.

George went to Cumberland to fetch his wife and daughter and return to Cumberland. On their way home, the weather turned bad as they crossed Martin's Mountain. Mary wanted to turn back to a farm they had passed. In trying to turn the carriage, the wheels slipped off the roadway and it went over a precipice. George jumped free, but Mary and the baby went over the hill with the carriage.

The baby landed uninjured in a pile of grapevines. Mary was alive but injured and bleeding.

His following actions were deemed suspicious or odd, at the very least, and they would come back to haunt him.

He left his injured wife where she was and cut the entangled horse free and let it run off. He then took up the baby and ran a quarter mile back to the nearest house. He left the baby there and asked for help for his wife. She was nearly dead by the time he returned for help. She remained under a doctor's care at the house for 10 days before being deemed strong enough to return to Cumberland.

George stayed with her a few more days before returning to Hagerstown. He wrote that his political opponents had spread rumors he had tried to kill his wife. "Had it been my design, I might have fully effected it, and not have been suspected in the least; and further, if so, Mary, who lived afterwards, might have disclosed it, which she never did," George wrote.

However, a short time after she returned to Hagerstown, Mary's father died, which sent her back to Cumberland.

It was during these absences of his wife that George admitted to "a few deviations from the path of pure living" beginning in 1826.

It was the following year, in June, that George met Rachel Cunningham. *The Intrigues, Amours, & Adventures of Rachel Cunningham,* a short pamphlet that mixes truth and fiction, describes her as possessing "those bewitching germs of beauty which won the favour and excited the admiration of all who beheld the superiority and contemplated the rising excellence of her charms."

George hired her to do washing and sewing for him since Mary was away so much, and he was busy running for sheriff. Rachel and George soon became lovers. *The Intrigues,*

Amours, & Adventures of Rachel Cunningham makes it clear that Rachel was the instigator of the relationship with George, "who affections she ensnared, in the first instance, by an artfully-managed stratagem purposely planned and practiced to entrap him."

A drawing of Rachel Cunningham from *The Intrigues, Amours, & Adventures of Rachel Cunningham.*

Rachel had fallen far in the world. She had been born in Philadelphia to a family that was wealthy enough to afford to send her to boarding school. However, her parents died by the time she was 14, and most of her father's money went to settle his estate. She wound up living with an aunt and uncle named Wallingdon in Bedford, Pennsylvania.

Because Bedford was a summer resort destination, Rachel's aunt and uncle made money renting rooms to visiting tourists. Also, as Rachel hit puberty, she grew into a desirable woman, whom men noticed.

"Mrs. Wallingdon soon found that with Rachel in the house, she could fill her rooms at double the rate. Rachel, as well, was quick to learn that she could trade her favors for jewelry and other lavish gifts," according to the website, Murder By Gaslight.

One boarder named Orlando Haverley, described as "a wealthy young gentleman of color," fell in love with Rachel, and she either fell in love with him or his money. When he left at the end of the season, she ran away with him.

They lived together but did not marry, and Haverley spoiled his lover with gifts until he caught her with another man, known only as Mr. G—. The two men dueled and Haverley lost his life.

Mr. G— took Rachel to Annapolis to live with him. When two sisters who were living with Mr. G— objected, he told them to move out.

Mr. G— also spoiled Rachel, but "after he refused to let her fire a servant, she tried to poison him," according to Murder By Gaslight. She didn't succeed, and Mr. G— came to his senses and sent her away.

She then moved around the mid-Atlantic as the lover of many men, including a Philadelphia judge and a wealthy merchant in Franklin County, Pennsylvania.

All this would seem to point to a woman of great beauty, but other reports paint her differently. "In point of personal attractions she was not to be compared to Swearingen's own modest, gentle and unassuming wife. Rachel was a large, gross, coarse, masculine woman, without a single attractive feature. Her character can be summed up in one word, she was a *wily* wretch," the *Alleganian* reported.

However, George's association with Rachel became known and was an issue during his campaign for the sheriff of Washington County in 1827. Because of his charm and family name, though, George won election handily. Among the many people vying for the office, George received 1822 of the 3775 votes cast.

This was the high point of his life, which soon took a darker turn.

Rachel runs away with her lover from *The Intrigues, Amours, & Adventures of Rachel Cunningham*.

How did the sheriff's wife die?

Washington County residents elected 27-year-old George Swearingen county sheriff despite rumors of an affair with a prostitute and another rumor that he had tried to murder his wife. The former was true, while the latter probably was not... at least at first.

With George's wife, Mary, spending a lot of time in Cumberland with her family, George spent a lot of time with Rachel Cunningham, a laundress and a prostitute. As her latter pursuits became better known, her landlord evicted her and kept any money she had already paid towards rent. He would "not suffer her to have the vegetables which she had raised and to which she was entitled," George wrote.

This only strengthened the attachments between the two as George started paying her rent for another home near the jail and promised to build her a home. George visited her regularly and was even with her on the night of his election.

However, George still suspected her of seeing other men, and she was. At some point, Rachel told George she was pregnant with his child. He didn't believe her and claimed she had been cheating on him. Distraught, Rachel tried to commit suicide by overdosing on laudanum. A neighbor found her and called for George, who in turn, tried to summon a physician.

"The physician he called to her relief refused to attend, swearing it would be better that she should die, that Swearingen was insane, and that he, the doctor, was too much his friend to do anything for her," according to *United States Criminal History*, published a few years after the murder.

George took matters into his own hands and forced her to take an emetic which saved her life.

Rachel admitted George wasn't the baby's father. She asked George to write the father a letter for her. He did, but he made the mistake of signing the letter with his own name out of habit. "Before the ink was dry, he perceived his error, ran his finger across the signature, to blot it, and signed her name over it. However, his name was still legible, and the letter was afterwards used to his damage, as were several others he wrote to her," according to *United States Criminal History*.

Despite her paternity lie, George still continued his affair, but now his infidelity was becoming common knowledge in the community. His father, his uncles, and leading men all urged him to break off his relationship, if not to save his marriage, then to save his career.

When Mary's mother learned of George's affair, she fetched Mary and brought her back to Cumberland. George didn't object since he didn't have to make excuses to spend time with Rachel.

Eventually, George built Rachel her own house and moved her into it. When a neighbor discovered his neighbor was a prostitute, he urged George to move her somewhere else because he feared she would set a bad example for his daughters. George refused to do so, and the neighbors became increasingly agitated by Rachel's presence that they decided to drive her out.

"The mob being about to demolish the house, he took her to his own, and kept her there five days for fear she should be torn in pieces," according to *United States Criminal History*.

He soon took her to a Charles Town, W. Va., tavern and left her there with money to live on. Then he traveled to Cumberland and told his wife he had sent her rival away. Mary agreed to return to Hagerstown with him. It is uncertain, even in George's confession, whether he meant this to be a break with Rachel and a new start with Mary.

If so, Rachel wasn't done with George. At the Charles Town tavern, she called herself Mrs. Swearingen and used the name to get invitations to dine with respectable families in the area. "For a while, the shameless played her part well, calling Mrs. Scott mother, and answering all questions touching the family with equal facility and assurance," according to *United States Criminal History*.

When the truth was discovered, George had to move Rachel once again, lest either she or the Charles Town residents cause more problems. After moving her around to different short-term homes, George put Rachel up at the Tevis Farm near Cresaptown, Md., and began visiting her again, often making the excuse to Mary that he was traveling on official business.

In September 1928, George went to Cumberland to bring his wife home from yet another visit with her parents. On the morning of Sept. 9, a young man driving cattle about a half mile from the Tevis Farm found George sitting beside his wife's dead body and cradling his daughter in his arms. George said his wife had been thrown from a horse and died when she struck the ground headfirst.

The coroner's inquest found that the knees of Mary's horse had been cut, probably in a fall. They ruled Mary "came to her death by act of Providence." She was buried in Cumberland.

Fate had cleared the way for George and Rachel to be together, but fate can be fickle.

The law man becomes a wanted man

In 1829, a coroner's inquest found Mary Swearingen, the wife of Washington County Sheriff George Swearingen, had died accidentally near Cresaptown. It was a tragedy, in particular, because Mary had been a mother with a young daughter, but these things happen and life continues.

For George, it was a gift because it allowed him to continue his affair with Rachel Cunningham with one less impediment.

This might have been the end of things, but Charity Johnson, who had helped prepare Mary's body for burial started telling people in Cumberland that Mary "had bruises on her throat, and other bruises that suggested she was violently raped," according to the website, Murder By Gaslight. She said Mary hadn't died in a fall from a horse. Johnson wanted the body disinterred and examined, but George refused, saying he didn't want his wife publicly exposed.

However, Mary's mother suspected Rachel had killed Mary. The place where Mary had died was about a half mile from where Rachel was living. Mrs. Scott asked for Mary's body to be re-examined, and George relented under public pressure. The doctors could not find anything conclusive from the decomposing body.

This did little to assuage George. He felt people in Cumberland would not let the matter drop. He also worried that because of Mary's mother's suspicions, people might harm Rachel. He rode to the Tevis Farm where Rachel was staying and had her pack. Then the both of them headed out for Canada on a single horse.

This move caused what George had been trying to avoid. It made people think that there was more to Mary's death than an accident. Doctors and lawyers examined what testimony and evidence they had. Despite not finding conclusive evidence on the body, the coroner's jury came back with a verdict, "That after a careful and full examination of numerous witnesses, they (the Jurymen) are of opinion that Mary C. Swearingen came to her death by the hands of her Husband, George Swearingen," according to the *Hagerstown Mail*.

Oddly, the big news that the Washington County Sheriff has murdered his wife and fled the state earned only three paragraphs in the *Hagerstown Mail* on Sept. 26. A general story about the U.S. Postmaster General and the work he did received three times as much space on the front page.

The Oct. 17, 1828, *Hagerstown Mail* carried three items on the same page pertaining to George Swearingen. The most important was the notice that Maryland Governor Joseph

Kent placed an $800 bounty (about $25,000 today) on George for his capture. The First Hagerstown Hose Company also excised George's name from its constitution created when the company formed, and the Mt. Moriah Masonic Lodge expelled George from membership.

Although they intended on heading to Canada, George and Rachel rode to Kentucky instead. They traveled at night, and George introduced himself as Campbell to anyone they met. When their horse gave out, George exchanged it for two ponies.

They made it to Kentucky but couldn't relax. A man in Elizabethtown recognized George, and another man recognized him in Owenville. They finally reached the George's relatives in the Green River Country where he hoped to rest. He told his relatives that Mary's death had been accidental and that he and Rachel were married. Neither was true, but his family believed him.

George wrote to his father asking for money. When a friend came from Maryland with the money, he also told George about the reward being offered for his capture. His father advised George to head to Texas (which was still part of Mexico at this time) alone because the authorities were seeking a couple on the run.

George took his father's advice, which upset Rachel. "They wept and embraced, and could not tear themselves apart," according to *United States Criminal History*, published a few years after the murder. "At last he told her that as she could not be happy without her child, his friend should go to Maryland for it and bring her and it after him. She replied that she did not care for the child, but was willing to accompany him without it. He objected that the danger of detection would be doubled should they travel together, bade her not to be uneasy, and promised not to forsake her entirely. He gave her money, kissed her, and at last they parted, his friend accompanying him to Shawneetown."

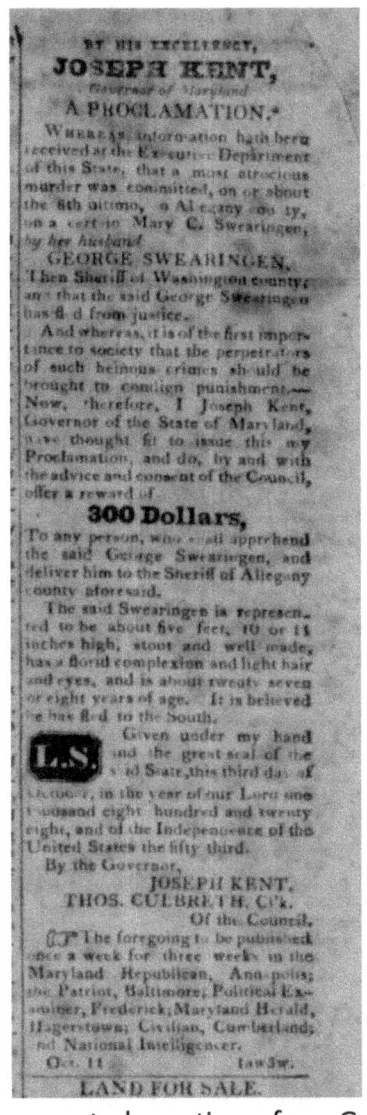

The wanted notice for George Swearingen offering a $300 reward.

The plan was for George to meet up with Rachel in New Orleans, and from there they would go to Texas. However, George was also recognized in New Orleans. The police hunted and captured him hiding on a ship. He spent two months in a jail "without a change of raiment, and covered in vermin," according to *United States Criminal History*.

While he was in jail, another prisoner told George that Rachel was in New Orleans searching for him. Then George made the odd decision to tell his jailer that Rachel was in town, so she could be arrested and they could be sent back to Maryland together.

They traveled by ship from New Orleans to Baltimore where they were transported to Cumberland, where George had been charged with murder. His would be the first murder trial in Allegany County.

Allegany County's first murder trial was sensational news

Washington County Sheriff George Swearingen's murder trial in Cumberland started on August 11, 1829. He was accused of murdering his wife a year earlier. He had attempted to escape the country, but the authorities captured him in New Orleans.

Some people also suspected George's lover, Rachel Cunningham, of having a hand in the murder, but there was not enough evidence to charge her. George also maintained that she was innocent in the matter.

During the trial in Cumberland, the prosecution aired every fact and rumor about George's life. The prosecution alleged that George had tried to murder his wife twice before, including the Martin's Mountain buggy accident. In the other incident, George supposedly tried to down his wife, Mary, in a river the day before she died.

"The first was probably a legitimate accident—Swearingen was a notoriously bad driver; the second, with no witnesses, was probably pure fiction," according to the website, Murder By Gaslight.

The prosecution also made the case that Mary hadn't been killed on the road where she had been found with George. George, according to the lawyers, had moved her there. "The strongest circumstance was, that Swearingen's horse and that of his wife were tracked into and out of a thicket close to the spot where the body was found. In the thicket a spot was trampled and stained with blood, and a club was found at hand," according to *United States Criminal History*.

The defense also floated some highly speculative theories. One was Mary had suffered from "leuco phlegmatic temperament." Defense attorney John McMahon argued this made Mary susceptible to spontaneous uterine hemorrhaging. "Her doctor had advised her to refrain from sex—explaining why George strayed in the first place," according to Murder By Gaslight. "The condition also explained why she appeared to have been raped before death. For good measure, he speculated that Charity Johnson had attacked the body with a broomstick to implicate Swearingen as a rapist."

During the closing arguments, Defense Attorney Price spoke for five hours and McMahon spoke to the jury for seven hours "making as able and as eloquent a plea probably as any speech ever made in a criminal trial in this State," according to the *Baltimore Sun*. Despite this, the jury only took 10 minutes to find George guilty of murdering his wife, and the judge ordered him to hang.

George was shocked. He didn't believe the prosecution had made its case. It wasn't that he had murdered his wife, it was he hadn't murdered her in the way upon which he had been convicted. From his jail cell, George dictated his confession and admitted he had killed Mary.

By his account, as he and Mary had neared the Tevis Farm, Mary had been insistent on seeing the tenants. He had tried to convince her otherwise, knowing Rachel was there. Mary finally let her husband know that her mother had told her Rachel was at the farm. The couple had argued, Mary turned her horse toward the farm. In anger, George hit her on the back of the head with all his strength, and she fell head first onto the road.

He dismounted and saw she was dead. With his daughter's cries confusing him, George sought to take the body to a stonier place before sounding the alarm. The body fell off the horse three times, accounting for some of the bruising. George also cut his wife's horse's knees with his knife to make it look like something has caused the horse to trip.

Unlike the prosecution's account, George insisted the murder hadn't been intentional, nor had he left the road at any time.

The execution took place on a flat area on the west side of Wills Creek near the courthouse. "He was escorted to the gallows by a number of companies of militia from adjoining counties and accompanied by a number of ministers of the Gospel," according to *The Sun*.

According to the *Annapolis Republican*, George was led from his cell to the gallows at 10 a.m. on Oct. 2. The militia companies were made up of six companies of soldiers, five from Bedford County and one from Somerset County.

"Being the first execution in Allegany county it drew an immense crowd of people from far and near, old and young. It could be called a tri-State gathering," according to the *Alleganian*.

His last words were that he was at peace with God and

the world and he had no fear of dying.

He was hanged at 11:40 a.m. Although it was not the first murder in Allegany County, it was the first execution.

"The strangest part of the matter was that his body, when it was cut down from the gallows, where it hung for an hour, was sent to the home of the mother of his murdered wife," *The Sun* reported.

Rachel Cunningham was not tried for any part she may have played in the murder, and she disappeared from history. However, the *Baltimore Sun* reported she is believed to have died in a Baltimore almshouse in 1869.

Flintstone Man Tries to Drive the Pentecostals Out

Enoch Alt, a 55-year-old Flintstone resident, didn't like it when the Pentecostal Church opened a church in Gilpintown. It wasn't a large church, but Alt was determined to drive the church and its members from the area.

In early February 1921, Alt and some friends attended a service at the church. The modern Pentecostal movement began at the turn of the 20th century when evangelist Charles Fox Parham started the Bethel Bible School in Kansas. He soon closed the school and began spreading his type of Christian faith. The church was not segregated, nor did it prohibit women from conducting ordinances. This did not sit well with many people and may have been the reason for Alt's hatred of the church.

David Walters was not a member of the church, but he attended one night to see what it was about. He left early because Alt kept yelling, "Cover your heads!" Fearing trouble, he left early. Asst. Rev. Johnson kept asking Alt and his friends to quiet down, but they wouldn't.

Then the church burned down at the end of the month. No one knew who did it, but Alt was suspected. However, without evidence, authorities couldn't charge him with arson. They did charge Alt, Dayton Dolly, Russell Dolly, Otis Bible, and Grant Bible with disturbing the church worship.

The trial in the circuit court drew a large crowd from Flintstone. Witnesses testified about Alt disrupting the service. Alt and Dayton were found guilty and fined $5 each (about $75 in today's dollars).

Alt refused to give up. Although the church building had burned, the members were still meeting in a storeroom.

On May 20, 1921, Rev. Walter Long was up early. He heard a car drive up and looked out his window in time to see a stick of dynamite thrown into his yard. "The minister ran out and picked it up, pursuing the fleeing auto party for several hundred yards in an endeavor to establish its identity," the *Cumberland Evening Times* reported. "He threw the bomb away and it exploded. Another bomb was set off in the barnyard adjacent to the Long home."

He also found another stick of dynamite under his porch and stamped out the burning fuse.

A similar attempt was made to dynamite the home of Gilpintown Pentecostal Church member Joseph Dolly, which also failed.

The bombers were not seen. All that was known was they had been driving in a Ford sedan.

Investigators immediately turned their attention to Alt because Rev. Long was the person who had reported Alt's disruption of church services to the police.

Neighbors told investigators they had seen Alt hiding dynamite that matched the description of the dynamite used in the attack on Rev. Long. They also verified that Alt hadn't gotten past having to go to court.

At the end of June, Sheriff Anthony Harvey and County Detective F. Clement Deneen arrested Alt and charged him with assault and intent to kill.

The jury found him guilty at the trial.

An Uninvited Guest Terrifies Families

Emory Troutman's young daughter was home alone in Gilpin when she heard a knock at the door. She opened the door and saw a stranger standing on the porch. He looked over her head into the house and then down at the girl.

"Are your parents home?" Joseph Zizaro asked.

"No, they won't be back until later," she told him.

He stared at her, saying nothing, then nodded to himself. "I called to murder your family, but since no one is home right now, I will have to put that off until they return."

Then Joseph turned and left, leaving a frightened girl behind.

"Zizaro had terrorized the people in the neighborhood of Pratt and Green Ridge for several days, going into people's homes with a drawn stiletto and ordering his meals prepared and if he felt sleepy a bed also," the *Cumberland Evening Times* reported in August 1901.

A family would sit down to eat, only to have Zizaro force his way into their home brandishing a knife. Then he would sit at the table with the family and eat a meal as if he was an invited guest. Women and children worried over whether they should leave their homes, in case they ran into the armed man. They wouldn't let their husbands and fathers go too far away from their homes, at least not without them.

While a Green Ridge farmer named Frank Murphy was out working in his fields, Zizaro forced his way into Murphy's home, brandishing a knife and pistol. He drove the Murphys out of the house and claimed it as his own.

Police finally caught up with Zizaro at the end of July 1901. Constable Kifer of Flintstone tried to capture the man on his own, but for a small man, Zizaro proved to be quite strong. Kifer called for help and several sheriff's deputies came to the area. It took four men to overpower Zizaro and handcuff him the next time Kifer tried to arrest the man.

While the lawmen were driving Zizaro to Cumberland and the county jail in a wagon, the Italian calmed down. He asked to have the handcuffs removed and promised he would go to jail without offering any resistance.

"He pleaded so pitiful that the officers finally complied with his request, but the handcuffs were no sooner off than Zizaro made an attempt to escape and had to be knocked down before he would surrender," according to the *Cumberland Evening Times*.

They delivered him to the jail in Cumberland where he faced charges for terrorizing residents. After interviewing him, Sheriff Martin told the newspaper the man was demented.

It is uncertain what happened to Zizaro, but he didn't show up in the newspaper stories again.

Lover's Triangle Ends in Murder

Two shots rang out in the early hours of a cold February 1900 morning in Borden Shaft.
"Oh my God, have mercy on me!" Owen Edwards, a 24-year-old Welshman cried out.

Although at least three people heard the cry, no one responded to it or seemingly cared.

"Owen Edwards went to his long account in the darkness and cold, while his successful rival sat a few yards away enjoying the society of the girl both men had coveted," the *Midland Press* reported.

One man lay dead in front of a house while his killer sat quietly inside the house talking and cuddling with his 17-year-old fiancée. While there was no question of who murdered whom, what no one was sure about was why it had happened.

Owen emigrated originally to Scranton, Pa., but he had moved to Carlos to work in the Western Maryland coal mines. He had only one relative in America. A brother captained a steamship that ran between Baltimore and Brazil. Owen boarded with Eli Williams in Carlos and was a member of several fraternal societies. His neighbors considered the Welsh miner quiet and sensible.

Owen became friends with Walter Wade, a former brakeman for the Cumberland and Pennsylvania Railroad, who became a driver for a Klondike coal mine. He lived with his parents in Borden Shaft, a couple hundred yards away from the home of Rosa Crowe and her father.

Rosa later said she had first met Owen when he and Walter visited her in her home. Although she said the visit didn't make much of an impact on her, it did for Owen. He became enamored with Rosa. However, Rosa was engaged to Walter.

Rosa attended a dance at Kenny's Hall with her fiancée. She was attractive and had plenty of men who wanted to dance with her, including Owen. However, she spent most of her time with Walter.

"During the ball both Wade and Edwards found time to drink rather heavily at the bar down stairs, and it is said that one was heard to threaten the other of a 'finish' before the night ended," according to the *Midland Press*.

Around 1:30 a.m., Walter and Rosa left the dance. Walter walked her to her father's home. Rosa's mother had died the previous year, so it was just Rosa and her father in the house. When Rose saw her father wasn't home, she asked Walter to stay until Jacob Crowe returned.

Owen had seen Rosa and Walter leave and followed them to the house. He watched the pair go inside and then the lights went out. His imagination ran wild.

"Then Edwards, who could not restrain his impatience to find out what was going on in the house, tried to find out. He stole through the garden gate, around the house and back, and at last went away for a few minutes. Wade and Rosa were watching him from the window, having promptly blown out the light on getting home. They claim that they had no idea who it was," the *Midland Press* reported.

For some reason, Owen took off his shoes as he came up the front walk. Walter picked up a rifle and fired high through the transom of the door.

Owen turned to flee. Rosa opened the door, and Walter fired out the door, hitting Owen in the back. He fell through the gate and died.

"Coolly setting the gun down, Wade returned to his love, and paid no further attention to his victim," the *Midland Press* reported.

Jacob Crowe returned home at 3 a.m. Walter was still at the home and told Jacob what had happened. Jacob took a lantern and walked outside to look at the dead man, "then returned to their occupations in the house, while the body stiffened in the cold night air," the *Midland Press* reported.

A few hours later, Walter sent a neighbor boy to get Constable E. E. Drew in Midlothian and gave himself up. Nickle's Undertakers came from Frostburg around 10:30 a.m. to take the body and prepare it for burial. Dr. Clymer examined the body and said death was instantaneous. The bullet severed Owen's spine and caused internal bleeding.

Clymer held a coroner's inquest to make an official determination.

Fannie Merrill, who lived in the other half of the double house where the Crowes lived, heard Owens call out after he had been shot, but she didn't hear the shots.

When Walter saw the rifle on display at the inquest, he pointed to it and said, "There's the gun that did the trick. It's a fine gun."

Rosa even showed the inquest panel the blood-stained grass "where Edwards had laid all the long night while she made merry with another man a few feet away, and remarked on the distance he had rolled after he was shot," the *Midland Press* reported.

In the end, it was decided that Walter should be tried for first-degree murder.

Was Owen Edwards murdered or not?

Walter Wade of Borden Shaft shot and killed Owen Edwards early on a frosty February morning in 1900. Then he walked back inside a house to continue his date with Rosa Crowe. Walter didn't even deny what he had done, and so the state's attorney charged him with first-degree murder.

When the trial started on April 26, 1900, certain details of the murder had changed, and the jury was left to decide who was lying and who was telling the truth.

State's Attorney Henderson presented the prosecution's case to the jury. He outlined the findings of the coroner's inquest. He said during the inquest, Walter said Edwards rattled the door trying to enter the house, Rosa opened the door, and Walter grabbed the rifle and shot through the open door.

"The door was closed and Miss Crowe and Wade went on with their conversation," the *Evening Times* reported.

When Jacob returned home at 3 a.m. and saw the dead body lying in front of his house, he rushed inside and asked, "What have you done?"

"I have shot at a man," Walter replied.

"Well, you have killed him," Jacob told him.

During the defense's opening statement, Mr. Richmond said that Walter and Owen weren't rivals for Rosa's affections. Walter and Rosa were engaged to be married. Walter and Owen were friends, and Walter had taken Owen to the Crowe house once when Walter went to see Rosa.

He explained that on the night of the murder, Walter and Rosa were inside the house and surprised at the sound of the gate being opened. At first, they thought Jacob was returning home, but when he didn't come inside, they called out. No one answered.

Rosa handed Walter the rifle, and he shot through the transom of the front door to scare off whoever might be outside. The person then tried to get in through the side door. They then opened the front door, saw a dark shape near the gate and shot above it. Mr. Richmond said Walter didn't know he had killed a man.

Henderson then presented the state's case.

Walter went home after the body was discovered and never even looked at it. The coroner's inquest jury found evidence of someone trying to enter the house, and they wondered why Owen hadn't been wearing shoes since there was snow on the ground in places, and it would have been uncomfortable walking on the cold, frozen ground in socks.

The Crowe house was a double house, and Walter's aunt lived in the other unit. She testified she heard a man cry out twice, but she thought it was a passing drunk. She didn't hear the shots, although she said she was a fairly light sleeper.

Henderson also pointed out that the coroner's inquest jury said that the bloody footprints found on the porch were from a dog and not Owen.

The prosecution called Rosa as a reluctant witness since she was the only witness. She said she had known Walter for nine years and they were to marry in July. She testified that during Owen's visit to her house with Walter, Owen had talked to her in the kitchen and urged her to "sack Walter." This happened about a month before the murder, but she said she never told Walter of the incident.

When the defense presented its case, Walter took the stand.

He said he accidentally shot out the door not in self-defense or defense of property. "I said to Mr. Crowe that I shot at a man; don't know why I said that; I never told [Jacob] Cephus Crowe that I shot at a man who was trying to get into the house; didn't try to find out who I killed," Walter testified.

However, he did not do himself any favors when he said he didn't shoot through the door. The gun supposedly went off accidentally.

Henderson then suggested that not only had Walter murdered Owen, but that Walter and Rosa staged the scene to get away with murder.

"They looked out the window and saw Owen Edwards, and then and there, Walter determined to get rid of him and he shot him and that was the end of it," Henderson said.

He pointed out that the couple testified Owen tried to get in the back door, but they shot through the front door. Also, why would people who said they were scared open the front door for any circumstances?

The jury deliberated seven hours and found Walter not guilty. He and Rosa were married a few months later.

Tragic Murder Remains Unsolved

It had been a great party beginning on Saturday night and Joan Charlton had truly enjoyed her last night alive.

Joan, a 19-year-old Frostburg State College student, didn't leave the party in Annapolis Hall until around 5:30 a.m. Sunday morning, September 11, 1983.

Somewhere between the party and her dorm room in Gray Hall, Joan was stabbed repeatedly in the chest and killed. Her nude body was left in a wooded area on the westernmost edge of the campus called the arboretum.

By 2 p.m. Sunday, when Joan still hadn't shown up, the Residence Life Office reported her missing. College police unsuccessfully searched the campus for her Monday.

On Tuesday, the Maryland State Police called in its crime scene search team to look for Joan in the arboretum. Shortly before 11 a.m., her body was found along the banks of Sand Spring Run, which runs through the arboretum.

Ray Presley with the Maryland State Police said the arboretum was the logical place to look. "She was last seen on one end of campus and she lived on the other end. It was likely she went through there," he said.

Within minutes, the area was swarming with police, including State Police Detective Sgt. John McGowan, head of the investigation division, County Criminal Investigator Donald Peck and Allegany County Sheriff's Deputy Fred Fadley.

A massive search of the area was begun to collect any evidence, locate witnesses and try to retrace Joan's last hours.

The state police crime lab, Medevac helicopter and K-9 units were also used for the search. Tfc. Carl Skidmore developed the search plan and directed the search.

Staff and 3,400 FSC students were nervous and worried. It had only been five years since a male student had been killed on campus and two years since four female students had been sexually assaulted.

Campus security was doubled from three officers overnight to six. Male students formed a volunteer escort service for women on the campus.

FSC President Nelson Guild said, "I am asking the Frostburg State College family to remain calm during this difficult time and to render assistance to law enforcement authorities. This is a tragedy for us all and you have my assurance that my staff and I will do everything possible to ensure the safety of students here at the college. Our prayers are with Joan's family and friends."

Police found Joan's laundry bag with clothes in it about 40 yards from her body. Her slippers were found near the bell tower. Police also sought information about a blanket that was related to the case.

More than 14 investigators sought information and interviewed possible witnesses, which numbered in the thousands.

Rumors said that the nine people who last saw her alive had something to do with her death.

"There's no way that you can convince me that if one of those nine had something to do with it, that the others could keep a secret for this long," said Presley.

Police also pursued leads as to whether the case was related to an Aug. 3 murder of a Goucher College co-ed in Towson.

"Both students were black, both females, both stabbed to death, both were found on a wooded campus and both cases are unsolved," said Emmet C. Burns with the National Association for the Advancement of Colored People.

Presley believes, "The murderer was someone passing through and the opportunity presented itself when he saw her walking past."

The case remains unsolved to this day, though it was included with about 80 other "cold" homicide cases that were given a fresh look by Maryland State Police in 2000.

CANAL LIFE

The Engineering Marvel Hidden Under a Mountain

On the day that construction began on the Chesapeake and Ohio Canal on July 4, 1828, the pressure was on the work crews to get dig the 184.5-mile-long ditch to Cumberland as quickly as possible.

Why the rush? The Baltimore and Ohio Railroad broke ground in Baltimore for its construction on the same day and Cumberland with its coal mines and agricultural products was the prize for both the canal and railroad. The first one to reach the city would be able to secure customers without competition until the other mode of transportation arrived.

The C&O Canal crews worked hard digging the canal and building 160 culverts, seventy-four lift locks and eleven aqueducts. However, the canal has only one tunnel—the Paw Paw Tunnel—and it was a major reason why the B&O Railroad beat the C&O Canal to Cumberland by eight years.

Construction

When planning the canal's route, it could have continued to follow the Potomac River through southeastern Allegany County, weaving along the Paw Paw Bends or cutting through a mountain. Following the river bends would have been the easier course, but cutting a tunnel through the mountain would save five miles and could be done in two years, according to the engineering estimates.

The C&O Canal Company chose the quicker route.

The contractor chosen to build the tunnel was a former Methodist minister named Lee Montgomery. He began hiring men to work on the tunnel in June 1836. The crews worked from either end of the tunnel digging into the mountain and from above cutting down into the mountain.

One of the portals of the Paw Paw Tunnel, which was supposed to save the C&O Canal time in its race to Cumberland, Md. Photo courtesy of National Park Service.

Workers sank four shafts into the mountain to work from above the mountain. The shafts were set in pairs; one shaft of each pair allowed for debris removal and the other was for ventilation. The northernmost pair of shafts was 122 feet deep and the southernmost pair of shafts was 188 feet deep.

The crews initially blasted away large areas of rock with black powder and then shaped the tunnel with picks and shovels. The rubble was hauled out of the tunnel with horse carts.

"The workers were not experts at blasting, and there was a great deal of overbreakage; the excavation was 40 percent larger than needed," Elizabeth Kytle wrote in *Home on the Canal*.

Once excavated, the tunnel arch was formed from layer upon layer of bricks. According to Kytle, the Paw Paw Tunnel lining is 13 layers of brick deep with some places having up to 33 layers. Any open spaces remaining above the arch were backfilled with the excavated material.

"The slaty rock was reasonably hard, but loose enough to make frequent trouble by caving in. It was dangerous work and it went at a snail's pace," Kytle wrote.

Montgomery had projected before construction began that his crews would be able to bore out seven to eight feet a day. The reality turned out to be that his crews working three shifts each day only managed 10 to 12 feet a week.

To complicate matters, work was suspended on the tunnel from 1842 to 1847 because of the C&O Canal Company's financial problems. Construction didn't resume until November 1848. It was completed by a different contractor, McCulloh and Day, and opened for navigation on October 10, 1850.

The final 3,118-foot-long tunnel is called "the greatest single engineering achievement on the canal," by the National Park Service. It is 22 feet wide and 24 feet wide and sheathed in more than 11 million bricks.

Operation

Though the Paw Paw tunnel was an engineering marvel, it was narrow for purposes of the canal. The canal was designed so that boats could pass each other going in opposite directions. The towpath and canal bed through the Paw Paw Tunnel were both only wide enough for one set of canal mules and one canal boat to move through the tunnel.

Because of the length of the tunnel, a canaller upon reaching one entrance of the tunnel could tell if another boat was already in the tunnel (if it was daylight), but it was impossible to tell if the boat was approaching or heading away. The canallers started lighting colored lanterns fore and aft on their boats to distinguish direction. A green lantern was hung fore and a red lantern was hung aft. That way, other canallers could tell whether boats in the tunnel were coming or going.

Leaving the Paw Paw Tunnel at its eastern end. Photo courtesy of the National Park Service.

If the boat was showing a green light, the canal boat captain knew that the boat was approaching and pulled over to wait.

Not that problems still didn't arise.

Some canal boat captains who were in a rush or just plain cranky, refused to yield the right of way to boats in the tunnel. George Hooper Wolfe tells one of the stories in his book *I Drove*

Mules on the C&O Canal.

Two captains—Jim McAlvey and Cletus Zimmerman—and their boats met in the middle of the tunnel. Neither man wanted to back up, and the captains got into a fist fight over who had the right of way. Then things escalated.

"A gun was drawn and would have been used but for the quick action of a mule driver who knocked the gun from the captain's hand into the Canal," Wolfe wrote.

Other boats began entering the canal from both ends of the tunnel and soon the tunnel was filled with boats. As day gave way to evening, crew members on the unmoving boats started corn cob fires in their cabin stoves to cook meals. Before too long, the tunnel began filling with smoke from the stoves and made staying in the tunnel very uncomfortable.

This sped up negotiations and the captains reached an agreement so that the boats could start moving again.

When traffic on the canal reached its peak during the 1870's, a watchman was hired to help regulate the traffic at the Paw Paw Tunnel and keep it from becoming a bottleneck. The watchman enforced the canal company rules for using the tunnel and could fine canal boat captains $10 for violating them.

The Tunnel Today

Even today, the Paw Paw Tunnel is still an impressive structure on the C&O Canal and it is still isolated. While there is a parking area just off Route 51 between Paw Paw, W.Va., and Oldtown, Md., visitors still have to walk about half a mile along the towpath to reach the tunnel.

A flashlight is recommended if you want to walk through the tunnel since it is quite dark and there is no interior lighting. It will also allow you to see some of the features of the tunnel, including the weep holes (openings in the brick liner that allow water to pass through), the rope burns on the wooden railing and the brass plates the serve as 100-foot markers inside the tunnel.

Healthy and energetic visitors can also hike a steep two-mile long, Tunnel Hill Trail, over the mountain. This trail passes by where the canal builders lived while the tunnel was being built.

The Murders That Didn't Happen on the Canal

Canallers were surprised one morning in the late 1890s as they exited the somewhat frightening Paw Paw Tunnel only to meet a sight of true horror.

The lockhouse at Lock 64 2/3 just below the east end of the tunnel was a charred mess. It had burned to the ground during the night, and it was probably just by luck that it hadn't started a forest fire.

The first canallers on the scene went ashore to search for the lockkeeper. He was a friendly man who lived alone in the house and tended the five locks—61, 62, 63 1/3, 64 2/3 and 66—at the east end of the tunnel.

Another lock had originally been planned in that group of locks, but financial difficulties forced the C&O Canal Company to drop the plan for Lock 65 and renumber the locks around it, which is why two of the locks had fractions in their number.

According to George Hooper Wolfe in his book, *I Drove Mules on the C&O Canal*, the lockkeeper "was found in the ruins, dead of burns and crushed skull, evidently murdered."

Because of the isolation in the area, word of the crime had to be sent back to Paw Paw, W.Va., which was the nearest town more than a mile away. From Paw Paw, a telegram could be sent to Cumberland to call the Allegany County sheriff to the scene. It all took the better part of a day.

Because of the difficulty required in reaching the lockhouse, the murderer had to know that something was there that he wanted.

Wolfe wrote that the lock keeper "was a collector of rare and unusual coins and delighted in showing them to Canal boatmen and anyone else interested. Many of the Canal boatmen would pick up coins for him as he was well liked by those who knew him."

The eastern end of the Paw Paw Tunnel. It was near here that a brutal murder was supposed to have occurred. Photo courtesy of the Library of Congress.

As search of the house's ruins showed that the lockkeeper's coin collection was missing, but the sheriff was unable to find a clue as to who had committed the murder.

"The incident was just about forgotten and people heard rumors that the affair was probably a local, well-planned inside job," Wolfe wrote.

However, the canallers were reminded each time they passed

through the tunnel locks of the friend whom they had lost. They also remembered some of the coins in the lockkeeper's collection. Some they had found for their friend and others were unusual enough to stick in their memories.

Months after the murder, some canallers were in one of the many saloons in Cumberland's Shantytown, closing the place down. A stranger walked in and offered to buy the canallers a drink, which they readily accepted. When the stranger paid for the drinks, he used a coin that the canallers recognized as one of the missing coins from the murdered lockkeeper's collection.

"The boatmen took the stranger in hand, searched him, and found other coins that had been shown to them by the locktender many times before. The boatmen handled him roughly and would have killed him on the spot had not the barkeeper interfered," Wolfe wrote.

Police were called to arrest the stranger. At his trial, canallers testified to which coins had come from the dead lockkeeper's collection and businessmen testified that the stranger had tried to pass other rare coins at their shops.

"On this evidence he was found guilty and hanged, maintaining his innocence, but finally admitting his guilt in the end," Wolfe wrote.

That's how the story goes of the murder on the C&O Canal, and thanks to the popularity of Wolfe's book, most people accept it as the truth. However, Wolfe wrote his book recalling his days on the canal in 1969 at age 75, and the real story didn't unfold quite the way he remembered it.

Trying to verify Wolfe's story is hard because it was vague. No names are given and only a decade is mentioned as a time frame for the murders. The C&O Canal park rangers don't believe the story, but they do tell a story of another murder on the canal that is better sourced.

"Lock tender Joe Davis and his wife were murdered here by shooting in 1934," Thomas Hahn wrote in his *Towpath Guide*. He expanded on the story in *The Chesapeake & Ohio Canal Lock-Houses & Lock-Keepers*, writing that Davis took care of Lock 61 in the last decades of the canal's operation. Hahn wrote that the bodies of Davis and his wife were burned after the murder to try and cover up the crime.

The first thing that caught my attention was the location of both murders. The two lockhouses were only 1.5 miles apart along an isolated section of the canal. What was the likelihood that three people were murdered and burned there?

Or was it five?

A canal boat passing through a lock. Photo courtesy of the National Park Service.

Searching the newspapers brings up a headline in the August 5, 1830, *Hagerstown Morning Herald*. It announced, "Two Believed Burned in Allegany Co. Home - FOUL PLAY IS HINTED AFTER SKULLS FOUND - Mystery Marks Home Burning And Disappearance At Kifer". This headline set the narrative that became the urban legend. However, the facts told a different story.

This turns out to be the Joseph Davis story, so Hahn has the year wrong in his account (which he admits is second-hand).

Joseph Davis and his wife were killed in a fire on Aug. 4. "They were found on the springs of a bed in the ruins of the house. Two skulls crumbled when touched," the *Morning Herald* reported. The fire was so hot that not only had the wood burned in the house but so had the locks and hardware.

Newspaper reports said that Mrs. Davis' name was Allie, but the 1930 census reported it as Ella. The newspaper accounts also vary on both of the Davis's ages. According to the 1930 census, Joseph was 59 and Ella was 53.

The Davis's bones were found in the basement of the house where they had fallen once the floor had collapsed. Ella Davis was identified by her wedding ring.

A neighbor, drawn by the smoke, found the ruins of the house the day after the fire and reported it to the authorities. The bones that were found were initially taken to Paw Paw, W.Va., which was the nearest town of any size. State's Attorney William Huster, Allegany County Sheriff W. H. Harvey and Coroner Joseph Finan came from Cumberland to investigate the case and determine what happened.

The newspaper also reported that casings from a small-caliber gun were found near the body.

Davis had been a lockkeeper at Lock 61 on the canal, but since the canal had shut down six years previously, he reported to the census that he was a farmer. It is not mentioned in the article whether he and Ella were still living in the lockhouse, but it is possible.

Though the murder story spread quickly through the community, the authorities quickly abandoned the idea.

"It had been rumored that the couple had met with foul play and their bodies burned in their home to conceal the crime. This was based on a report that old coins which Davis collected and had under glass in a frame was missing. The officers, however, found a five-dollar gold piece and the metal of twelve silver coins, which had melted," the *Hagerstown Daily Mail* reported on the afternoon of Aug. 5.

The story of the missing coins is similar to Wolfe's story.

Finan announced on Aug. 6 that Joseph Davis had been smoking, probably a pipe, and may have fallen asleep. A spark from the house caught the house on fire. No foul play was suspected.

Even this story has evolved. When I originally published the story in 2013, it was a recounting of the Wolfe story. Then at the urging of Karen Gray, a C&O Canal historian, I looked into the Davis murder and was able to reconcile the two stories.

In 2015, Gray wrote me that she had found another murder that seemed to tie into the canal legends.

In 1900, William McCully lived along the canal near the eastern end of the Paw Paw Tunnel. Although this is where Locks 61-66 were located, McCully was not a lockkeeper. He ran a mercantile business near the tunnel that catered to canallers.

When McCully died in 1903, the *Cumberland Evening Times* reported, "About three years ago the deceased and his aged wife were the victims of horrible treatment by a gang of robber, who, after tying them both with rope, applied torches to their feet until they revealed where a considerable sum of money was hidden."

When the couple was discovered the next morning, it was thought that they would die. Mrs. McCully never did recover fully from the robbery and died three months later.

Sound familiar? Robbers stealing money and the use of fire. Wolfe's story now seems a poor recollection that combines the McCully and Davis stories although there are significant differences between this story and the others. There was no murder and no arson, the location and date would suggest that it influenced the legend of the canal murder.

"This has got to be one of the best examples of how legends reflect and rework true or likely true information from diverse sources," Gray wrote to me.

Forging Through the Mountains

When the Chesapeake and Ohio Canal finally opened to Cumberland, Md., in 1850, the canal directors still talked of continuing on to the Ohio River so that boats could travel from Washington, D.C., to Pittsburgh, Pa. This was the ultimate goal of the canal, which is why it was named what it was.

However, nothing ever came of finishing the canal, and it closed in 1924. A few years later, the U.S. Army Corps of Engineers took another look at the canal and the Potomac River.

At the beginning of 1938, it was announced that the Army Corps of Engineers had completed its survey of the river and its tributaries "for a proposed canalized waterway from Washington to Cumberland and connecting with the Ohio River at Pittsburgh with tidewater," according to the *Oakland Republican*.

The C&O Canal had been closed for 14 years at this point and had fallen into disrepair, with lock doors missing, the berm damaged, and trees growing in the canal. In addition, in its final years, the canal had been too narrow and shallow for the increasing size of cargo ships.

The Army Corps of Engineers survey decided not to use the existing canal but to turn the Potomac River into a navigable waterway. It was revealed that to canalize the Potomac River to Cumberland would require 27 dams, "four of them to be power-navigation dams capable of supplying 1,000,000,000 kilowatt hours of prime power annually," according to the newspaper.

The C&O Canal in Georgetown after it had closed. Photo courtesy of the Library of Congress.

The construction cost was estimated at $60 million ($1.01 billion in 2017 dollars). This would also pay for creating a twelve-foot-channel in the Potomac River from Washington, D.C. to Cumberland. "A nine-foot water-way tunnel is proposed under the mountains to the Youghiogheny river, then through three locks and dams to the mouth of that stream at McKeesport with the Monongahela River," according to the newspaper.

The tunnel, which would have started near West Newton, Pa., was declared feasible and a better alternative than building a series of locks and dams to take canal boats up and over the mountains.

Engineers worked out of Cumberland and Eastern Garrett County in Maryland for a number of years looking at factors such as navigation, water power, flood control, and irrigation.

Four routes leaving Cumberland on existing waterways were considered. These were Will's Creek and the Casselman River; Savage River via Piney Creek or the Casselman River; Deep Creek and the Youghiogheny River; or the North Branch Potomac River and Youghiogheny River.

Once the engineers' report was released, businesspeople to the west of the mountains began considering its possibilities as well as the politicians in these areas. In particular, coal and iron producers in the Pittsburgh area studied the proposed plan. It would offer them a new way to get their products to Washington, D.C.

Politicians to the west of the mountains supported the idea and a hearing was scheduled. The Western Pennsylvania politicians urged businessmen and citizens to attend and voice their opinions. They released a statement that read, in part: "The present fate of this much needed improvement rests with those in Western Pennsylvania, who are vitally interested."

Despite the initial interest, the plan eventually stalled before any further money was allocated.

In part, this was due to the fact that by June of 1938, an agreement was reached whereby the Baltimore and Ohio Railroad sold its holdings in the canal to the Public Works Administration, which in turn, would give the property to the National Park Service.

"It is understood that the national park services plan to use the right of way for scenic highway, as far west as Great Falls, and eventually all the way to this city," *The Cumberland Evening Times* reported.

This was the plan until U.S. Supreme Court Justice William O. Douglas hiked the towpath with a group of citizens and reporters in 1954 in an effort to save the C&O Canal. The hike changed the opinion of some of the newspaper editors who had been supporting the parkway.

In 1971, the C&O Canal finally became a National Historic Park.

When Coal Was King

Maryland Government Goes Into the Mines

After the Maryland Legislature passed a new law in 1876, it fell on Peter Cain to inspect Western Maryland's coal mines for the first time and report back what he found in 1877.

The politicians passed the law because of the growing number of men employed in the mines and the importance the trade was becoming to Maryland's economy. Cain noted that there was a need for "directed attention to a more careful and uniform system of mining and has suggested the propriety and necessity for the enactment of laws, looking as well to the protection of the health, safety and lives of the miners, as to the vast interests represented by the coal trade of these counties."

During his inspection of the Allegany County mines, Cain began his tour with the Consolidation Coal Company Mine in Hoffman Hollow and ended with the Hampshire and Baltimore Company Mine. He would introduce himself to the mine foreman and then enter the mine, noting things like the opening, ventilation, and supports.

"During such inspection, whenever it was apparent that a change ought to be made in any particulars in the mine, either of placing props, changing water courses or adjust any apparatus connected with the mine, the officers in charge acted promptly upon my suggestion and set about removing the objectionable matter or making the correction suggested. These requests, so made, I am pleased to say, with but two exceptions, cheerfully complied with," Cain wrote.

He found the miners more reluctant to talk. They were probably afraid that if they said anything negative about the mine or how it operated, it would get back to the mine owner who would punish the miners.

The Appleton Mine in Lonaconing. Courtesy of the Albert and Angela Feldstein Collection.

The first thing that Cain noted was the mines were properly ventilated. "In most of the mines on Georges Creek there are headings that run entirely through the mountain, entering it on one side and coming out so to speak to daylight on the other side. In such mines no air shafts are needed, the headings affording an ample current of pure air, sufficient for thorough ventilation," Cain wrote.

He also said that Mount Savage was "honeycombed with openings." Miners lowered the coal that came out of those mines to the dumphouses on the railroad.

As he moved into Georges Creek, he said the towns were busy with "an air of thrift and industry." He noted the good living conditions in the town with churches, schools, and stores. The miners lived in comfortable homes.

He wrote that the mines were created using the room and pillar system. Miners "excavate a horizontal slot from one side of the room to the other." This is known as "the undermining" and it is 3- to 4-feet deep.

"If he is at all afraid that a part of the breast may fall before he gets the slot entirely finished for the width of the room, he puts some wedges as he goes on with the slot," Cain wrote.

Then vertical slots are cut into the wall that are 8 to 10 wide called "shearings." Once these are done, the miners knock the wedges out of the undermining and drives iron wedges near the roof line. "The mass of coal which he had undermined and sheared, and which was held only in place by its adhesion to the roof and to the solid body of coal in front of it," Cain wrote.

The miner then breaks up the debris to get the coal as free from dirt and stone as possible before he tosses it into the coal car. When the cars were full, mine ponies pull them to the surface.

This first annual report was the first look into how coal mines operated in Western Maryland. It was such an important report that not only was it given to the Maryland Legislature, it was printed in the *Daily Cumberland Alleganian and Times.*

In Coal Blood

Word spread during the 1922 coal strike in Western Maryland that the Consolidation Coal Company brought in a "gunslinger" to protect the strikebreakers whom the coal company brought in from out of state to try to keep their mines open. Even the striking coal miners had to admit that their replacements were friendly and nice, but that didn't stop the miners from hating them because of what the strikebreakers represented. Some merchants wouldn't sell to strikebreakers to show their support for their local miners.

One of those places was Chabot's Store in Eckhart Mines. It was a popular place in the summer because Ed Chabot sold delicious 1-, 5-, and 10-cent cones. Joe Drum, a young boy, walked down one day for a cone and found the place very busy and noisy. Joe had to speak loudly so that Ed could hear what flavor he wanted. Ed dipped out the ice cream into a cone.

"As Ed started to hand me my cone, I suddenly became aware of a terrific silence in the room," Joe recalled in a newspaper article years later. "I saw an expression of horror in Ed's face. I felt scared."

Joe took his cone and turned around. There stood the gunslinger. It was an appropriate name for him. He dressed like a cowboy with leather chaps, leather vest, leather boot, and a large hat. More importantly, he wore a large gunbelt and carried a pistol in the holster.

"I want a pack of Camel cigarettes," the gunslinger said.

Ed had taken a stand to support the miners, he couldn't very well sell to the company man without losing face in front of the many miners in the store.

"We don't sell to strikebreakers!" Ed said sharply.

The gunslinger's eyes narrowed, his lips pressed into a tight line, and his expression hardened. He put his hand on his pistol and loosened the loop that held it in place.

"Mister, I want a pack of cigarettes, and I'd just as soon shoot you as look at you," the gunslinger said. "Now, I want those cigarettes."

Ed reluctantly picked up a pack of Camels and passed them to the man. The man paid for them and then turned and left.

"I can see Ed, red faced and in agony, reaching down for the cigarettes, very clearly to this day," Joe wrote.

Ocean Mine in Midland. Photo courtesy of the Albert and Angela Feldstein Collection.

The miners forgave Ed, but the gunslinger's action had their desired effect. The Eckhart merchants started selling to the strikebreakers.

Trying to unionize

The 1922 coal miners' strike was a national strike that grew from the miners' grievances against the powerful coal companies. A regional strike in southern West Virginia in 1921 had turned into a bloody battle. The Battle of Blair Mountain was the largest labor uprising in the United States. About 40,000 miners, coal company men, and soldiers fought for more than a week. In the end, around 130 people were killed.

While it was a union defeat, it did not end the United Mine Workers' grievances against the coal company, and the union called a nationwide strike on April 1, 1922. Although not unionized the Western Maryland miners also walked out to support their fellow miners.

Coal was the lifeblood of Georges Creek for decades and the region produced some of the best coal in the world. Maryland coal production peaked in 1907 with 5.5 million.

"In 1920, just before the onset of postwar depression, the Georges Creek mines produced roughly 4 million tons and employed about 5,500 miners. This was the last of the good years for the region," wrote Kathryn Harvey in *The Best-Dressed Miners*.

The Maryland miners were reluctant to strike for two major reasons.

Nationally, many coal mines had low pay and poor working conditions, though according to Harvey, the Allegany County miners "were said to be generally satisfied with their wages and working conditions." However, Harvey notes different companies underpaid their miners for the amount of coal they mined by using light scales. The miners were earning between $6.40 and $7.20 a day. The union was pushing for $7.50 a day.

The other reason was that the unions had failed to unionize the Maryland mines in the past. Previous attempts had been made in 1879, 1882, 1886, 1894 and 1900 to unionize the mines.

"Unions, however, had failed to establish a secure base in the county. Although a large number of miners and a smaller number of laborers and mechanics were sympathetic to unionization, company policy still held sway. Determined to retain their authority, moreover, mining companies would mount a more vigorous counteroffensive against union in the last decade of the nineteenth century," wrote Harry Stegmaier, Jr. in *Allegany County-A History*.

Armed miners in West Virginia during the 1922 coal strike. Photo courtesy of Wikimedia Commons.

Miners even distrusted other miners. During the 1882 strike, the National Knights of Labor didn't financially support striking miners, which weakened the miners' ability to continue striking. County miners remembered this when the

1894 strike call came and some miners refused to strike because they feared the union wouldn't financially back them.

The local strike

During this strike, Stegmaier wrote, "The division among Allegany miners became a bitter one, involving 'the gentle sex' in not-so-gentle modes of action. Eckhart women accompanied their husband to the mines and threatened to replace men forced out of the mines by strikers. On the other hand, Carlos sisters stoned workers coming out of the tunnels. Frostburg miners encountered sixty women 'armed with tin pans, buckets, baseball bats and babies' as they returned home to work."

Consolidation Coal kicked striking miners out of company housing, and brought in strikebreakers Cleveland, Pittsburgh and West Virginia to keep the mines open. The companies also brought in guards armed with automatic weapons and even submachine guns, according to Stegmaier.

Extending the strike

When the national strike ended August 15, the Allegany County miners stayed out in an effort to win union recognition. The UMW supported the strikers with $750,000 and a food commissary in Frostburg.

Stegmaier wrote, "This explosive situation was further complicated when many of the local miners who did not agree with continuing the strike went back to work. Strikers threatened reprisals against them and their families. Violence was bound to occur, and it soon did."

In August 1923, Harry Martin, a Consolidation Coal Company mine guard, was charged with throwing a grenade into a crowd of picketers.

Later that month, George Porter of Zihlman was shot and

killed while driving his motorcycle to work at a Mount Savage and George's Creek Coal Company mine. W.H. Walbert of Consolidation Coal Company was eventually charged with the murder.

Walbert was also shot in the incident. He was taken to Miner's Hospital for treatment, but according to the *Cumberland Evening Times*, "it was decided later to remove him to Cumberland as there is said to have aroused much feeling over the shooting of Porter and [Walbert] might run afoul a mob." He went to Western Maryland Hospital where he stayed under guard.

In another incident, Frank Miller of Gilmore was shot and wounded while driving to work at a mine. Martin was also charged in this shooting. Unknown assailants later fired shots into his house. "At this particular point, it is declared by eyewitnesses, there was a volley [of shots]," reported the *Cumberland Evening Times*.

In September, 300 striking miners attacked a much smaller group of strikebreakers heading to work. Later that month, striking miners shot four strikebreakers in Barton.

Stegmaier wrote, "Violence became so prevalent that the Allegany County grand jury, after considering the numerous cases of assault and intimidation, recommended that a special constabulary be formed to preserve order. The grand jury described conditions, particularly in Frostburg and Midland, as 'a disgrace to the county.'"

The UMW called off the nearly 20-month strike in November 1923 without unionizing the mines.

The last incident of mob violence against a strikebreaker during the strike happened in Frostburg in late 1923, according to a story in the *Frostburg Sesquicentennial Souvenir Book*. A group of striking miners saw a strikebreaker in town. They yelled, "Scab!" at him.

The strikebreaker ignored them until they shot at him. The man ran down Main Street and turned onto Maple Street. He jumped on a motorcycle he had hidden in a barn earlier in the day and escaped the mob.

Unionizing

Even after the strike ended, many of the striking miners weren't rehired because they had showed their union sympathies. The strike had also happened at a time when demand for coal was decreasing, and the combination of the two crippled the coal industry in Maryland.

"Even though organized labor did not cause the ruin of the Georges Creek coal region, it is nevertheless undeniable that the miner's strike of 1922-23 hastened the end," Stegmaier wrote.

Between 1923 and 1930, 27 mining companies went out of business in the Georges Creek Region. Even the union suffered, losing over 60 percent of its membership in the region by the end of the strike.

It wouldn't be for another decade or so that the UMW gained a foothold in the state, and it was because of the Wolf Den Coal Company miners in Shallmar in Garrett County. The striking coal miners picketed the company store and blockaded the road to the mine. People feared it might turn into another 1922 strike. The coal companies might have held out, except that Shallmar Coal Company was the weak link. Mine owner Wilbur Marshall came down from New York on one of his infrequent trips and signed a contract with the union. He was the first of the Maryland mines to do so and the rest soon followed his lead.

Miners working in a coal mine. Photo courtesy of Whilbr.org.

Rats Fleeing a Sinking Ship

The 1922 national coal strike was a trying time for all parties involved - miners, coal companies, local businesses, and... rats.

"It is estimated that 25,000 mine rats, unable to live in the deserted mines of the Georges Creek region are infesting the farms and mining communities in Eckhart, Barton, Hoffman, Grahamtown, Morantown, Allegany, Barrellsville, and many sections down the Creek," the *Cumberland Evening Times* reported on August 12, 1922.

Most of the coal mines in the county had been idle since April 1 when John L. Lewis called a nationwide strike. Although Allegany County mines weren't unionized, the miners walked out in sympathy.

Mine rats lived on the scraps they could steal from miners' lunch pails and other refuse. The industriousness of the rats was one reason the miners brought their lunches in metal pails rather than paper bags. However, some rats were also clever enough to figure out how to get into the pails.

The rats also used hay and straw meant for mules and ponies housed underground to make their own nests. The newspaper reported that each coal mine was home to an average of 1,000 rats.

While the rats were generally unwanted companions in the coal mines, some miners saw a benefit in having them around. "Now we all know that the mine rat was a favorite of the miners, the miners shared their lunch with them, they chased them, talked to them on occasion, and we all know that they saved many a miner's life. If you saw the rats running out the gangway it was a good idea to follow them, they had an uncanny ability to detect danger, actually they found out rats like many other animals are able to feel seismic changes," according to Coal Region History Chronicles website.

The strike gave the rats another reason to leave the mines. They were hungry.

The *Cumberland Evening Times* reported farmers and gardeners in the coal region were complaining that rats were ravaging their gardens and chickens. The rats ate corn, cabbage, tomatoes, and young chickens.

"The rat's choice of edibles seems to be corn," the *Cumberland Evening Times* reported. "On one farm near Shaft, one complete row of corn has been destroyed by the pests."

One woman reported she found a chicken with its head gnawed off. "The chicken had evidently caught its head in the wire of the coop and during a struggle to free itself, 'Mister Rat' took advantage of its plight and had enjoyed a chicken dinner," the newspaper reported.

Other farmers reported their chickens had parts of their wings and feet missing, which was attributed to attacks from mine rats.

The rats had apparently been living well underground. Reports were some of the rats emerging from the mines were "as large as five-months-old cats and their capacity for destruction is unlimited."

Until mid-August, the rats had only been reported on the farms in mining town, but reports had come in of people in those villages finding the rats in their basements.

With so many rats now showing themselves, striking miners began honing their shooting skills. They hunted the rats and when they found them, they started shooting. By August, miners had shot 87 rats. Women took a more-clandestine approach, setting traps and putting out poison to try and keep their homes rat-free.

Once the strike ended in 1923, any rats still alive in Georges Creek returned to familiar and safer territory below ground.

Miners descending into a coal mine. Photo courtesy of Wikimedia Commons.

ODDS & ENDS

A New County From Allegany and Garrett

Garrett County wasn't even a decade old when word started spreading that there was a move afoot to slice out a western portion of Allegany County and eastern portion of Garrett County to form yet another new county in Western Maryland.

"For a number of years past a few individuals living in Frostburg and vicinity have been agitating the question of carving a new county our of parts of Allegany and Garrett counties—for what purpose has never been definitely states, unless it is to create more offices. It certainly cannot be said the Georges Creek region has not a full share of offices in Allegany county at this time," the *Alleganian and Times* reported in 1878.

It had reached the point that freshman legislator Joseph Benson Oder, a Democrat on the Allegany County delegation in the House of Delegates submitted a bill that many believed, if passed, would form a new county.

Garrett County was formed in 1872 from the westernmost end of Allegany County and the newspaper noted, "Allegany has been divided, and we venture to say if the people of Garrett had the privilege of voting again on the subject they would gladly return to their former allegiance."

The *Alleganian and Times* clearly came down on the side

that it was a bad idea. The newspaper article pointed out that Allegany County had very little debt at the time and that taxpayers had paid for and built all of the necessary public buildings at great expense. Some of those citizens would be living in the new county. Forming a new county not only meant that new public buildings would need to be constructed in a new county seat (which most likely would have Frostburg), but residents of the new county would have to pay their pro rata share of the existing Allegany County debt.

Not even the potential residents of the new county were pleased with what was happening.

A Frostburg resident wrote to *The Mining Journal* criticized the decision saying, in part, "Ye Frostburg lunatics, if you are submerged, ye Lonaconing lunatics, must go down with the 'All for truth.'"

The *Alleganian and Times* went so far as to suggest that the new county move wasn't so much something to benefit the citizens, but a way to create more government jobs "for the especial benefit of men too lazy or too ignorant to make a decent living for themselves?"

Oder, who was the former editor of *The Mining Journal*, finally wrote to the *Alleganian and Times* to try and explain his bill.

"Hence, I am amazed that both the measure alleged and myself have been so grossly misunderstood by an intelligent community," Oder wrote.

He said the bill was actually a Garrett County bill proposed by the Garrett County delegation, not Oder.

"It provides for the passage of certain local laws of Allegany county in force at the time of division, but never re-enacted for Garrett county," Oder wrote. "In framing the title of the present bill it was necessary to *quote* the title of the act of 1872, which provided for the 'formation of a new county,' etc. That is all." He added that the bill was "harmless."

Harmless or not, it went through three readings and was never introduced in the House of Delegates, which may have been due in part from the public outcry.

Oder served only one term in the Maryland House of Delegates from 1878 to 1880. He was a native Virginian, who had fought in the Civil War as a Confederate soldier and was present at the battles of Cold Harbor, Malvern Hill, Chancellorsville, Winchester, and Gettysburg. According to J. Thomas Scharf's *History of Western Maryland.*

The fellow members of the Allegany County delegation during Oder's term were William Brace, Jr. (R), Patrick Carroll (D), and William McMahon McKaig (D).

The Last of the Crow Wolves in Cumberland

Official records call him Frank Parks, but his name was Ti Kar Nak, meaning "Bent Knife" in the language of the Crow Indians. He was one of the last of the legendary Crow "Wolves," scouts for the U.S. Army.

Born in the Greasy Grass country of Montana, in the foothills of the Pryor Mountains, in 1895, Ti Kar Nak was the son of another Crow Wolf named Mee Na Tsea No or "White Swan." Mee Na Tsea No scouted for Gen. George A. Custer and was wounded at the Battle of Little Bighorn in 1876. Mee Na Tsea No was chasing a Blackfoot warrior on horseback. They fired at each other at the same time and were wounded. They fell from their mounts, but despite being hit twice, Mee Na Tsea No killed the Blackfoot. However, Mee Na Tsea No's wounds left him crippled. When he died in 1905, Mee Na Tsea No was buried in the National Cemetery at the Custer Battlefield in Montana.

Following in the footsteps of his father, Ti Kar Nak enlisted in the army at age 17 in 1907. He scouted for Gen. John "Blackjack" Pershing along the Mexican border as they hunted for Pancho Villa. When Ti Kar Nak was discharged from the U.S. Army in 1915, he went to Canada to enlist with the British Army and fight in World War I.

He saw action for the first time on Easter Sunday 1915. His commanders used his scouting skills and often teamed him with a Gurkha from India.

"These two teamed up on night patrols into the German lines and were cited numerous times for their work in wreaking havoc with the morale of enemy troops manning outposts," the *Cumberland Evening Times* reported. "They worked always at night, each armed with his favorite knife. They were quiet and deadly."

Ti Kar Nak with students during a school visit. Scanned from the *Cumberland Times-News*.

The pair had orders to strip any bodies of all papers and to bring back a shoulder epaulet of each person to use for identification purposes. However, the Germans were also issued cigars, which they kept in a pouch behind their left shoulder.

"I tell you, we had a pretty good supply of cigars," Ti Kar Nak said during an interview.

He was caught in a gas attack and sent to a hospital in England for treatment. He was in London when the first Americans arrived to fight in the war. He transferred back to the U.S. Army and was assigned to the A Company, 301st Tank Battalion. His job lay out route for the tanks around mine fields and marshes, and he had to do this while being shelled and shot at.

Years later, Lt. Thomas H. Miller, an officer who served with Ti Kar Nak, wrote "You were quiet and a good influence on the company, and in action there wasn't a more reliable man in the whole outfit."

While laying out a tank path, Ti Kar Nak was wounded a second time. "His wounds were so serious that the spent five years in military hospitals; he still carries a piece of steel so near his spine that doctors have never been able to remove it," the *Cumberland Evening Times* reported.

Once he recovered, he performed limited duty teaching survival skills, hand-to-hand combat, and knife fighting to soldiers.

He left the service in 1935 and took over heading security for Davison Chemical in Baltimore. When the U.S. entered World War II, Ti Kar Nak tried to enlist, but he was a 46-year-old who still carried shrapnel from his wounds. He was turned down.

Then the Army over the chemical plant in 1942 because of military value, and Ti Kar Nak began training MPs.

He retired in 1960 and started enjoying his hobbies more. He would bead wampum belts, talk to school kids, and write poetry.

He came to Lavale to live with his granddaughter Diedre Clemons who was a substitute teacher and tutor.

When he was interviewed in 1969, he said that he was still willing to fight for his country. "I am old but not too old yet to take up my ax and knife to protect what is mine, what my ancestors fought to give me and what I want those who come after me to have, to hold and to love," he said.

When he died on August 25, 1982, the *Cumberland Times-News* called him a "true American." He is buried in Hillcrest Memorial Park.

Frostburg Firemen Answer the Call

When fire destroyed 40 businesses and residences in Frostburg on September 5, 1874, residents began thinking it was about time that Frostburg had its own fire company.

The fire had started in the loft of the Beall and Koch store on Union Street at 12:20 p.m. and it probably could have been contained to that building if a serious effort could have been made to drown the flames. It wasn't, though. Residents didn't have the ability to mount much more than a bucket brigade.

The fire spread along Union Street, Broadway, Mechanic Street and Water Street. Keller's Store, Franklin Block, Marx Wineland's store and Hoblitzell Stables "being very dry structures, were in a few minutes a sheet of flames," according to the *Frostburg Mining Journal*.

A call for help went out, but the fire engines from Cumberland didn't arrive until 3 p.m. to put out the fire. Total losses from the fire were 40 businesses and homes totaling $149,900 (about $2.7 million today).

The damage from that fire that was caused by a delay in response started the citizens of Frostburg thinking that they needed their own fire company so they wouldn't have to depend on Cumberland's horse-drawn engines to arrive from 10 miles away.

And so, on March 18, 1878, a group of men met in the Frostburg city council chambers and organized themselves into a fire company of 35 members. George Wittig was named the first chief and George McCulloh was the first company president.

Former Frostburg Mayor Joseph Baer dressed in his Frostburg Fire Department uniform. Courtesy of the Frostburg Museum.

Though independently formed, the company expected the mayor and city council to help support the company with funds from the city treasury.

The *Frostburg Mining Journal* printed some tongue-in-cheek advice to the new fire company members on March 30. When the alarm sounds: "The moment you hear an alarm of fire, scream like a pair of panthers. Run any way, except the right way – for the furthest way around is the nearest way to the fire." Barn fire priorities: "Should the stable be threatened, carry out the cow-chains. Never mind the horse—he'll be alive and kicking; and if his legs don't do their duty let them pay for the roast. Ditto as to the hogs;--let them save their own bacon or smoke for it."

The following day, the company performed its first drill on the streets of Frostburg. The alarm was sounded at 3 p.m. and the men hurried to the hose house on Water Street from their homes around the city. The hose carriages were dispatched to the Gross and Nickel's furniture shop on Main Street where they were able to attach the hose to a fire plug and throw water within 4 minutes of the alarm.

On April 6, the *Frostburg Mining Journal* announced, "Hereafter, in case of fire, the large bell in St. Michael's Church steeple will be tolled, instead of three being rung as for church related matters."

The company now had its manpower, equipment, hose house and alert system in place. One final administrative piece came on December 9, 1878, when the Frostburg Fire Department received its charter.

The Frostburg Fire Company has grown to two stations with more than 70 volunteers today who are on call around the clock to protect their families, friends and neighbors.

The First State-Supported Hospital in Maryland

In the early part of the 20th century, a miner's trip to get emergency care in Allegany County was nearly as hazardous as working in the coal mines. It meant a long trip over rough and winding roads to Cumberland. It seemed obvious that a hospital was needed in the mining region of the county." Such a hospital is much needed, for men are being injured in the mines of this region every day. They are jolted home on stretchers or in wagons, and must await the arrival of the family physician, and do with such care and nursing as can be given them by the women of the family. With three coal miners from this county in the House of Delegates, it is reasonable to expect that something will be done towards the founding of a hospital on George's Creek," the *Cumberland Evening Times* reported in 1908.

It wasn't until 1913 that something was finally done about it. Miner's Hospital in Frostburg opened its doors in November 1913.

"The institution is unquestionably a credit to the state, county, town and hundreds of good people who have contributed. It is a long felt want splendidly supplied," the *Cumberland Evening Times* reported.

When the hospital first opened its doors, patients saw rooms with an iron bed, mahogany dresser, rocking chair and bouquet of pink and white carnations. Ernestine Wittig had placed the bouquets in all of the rooms for the opening. The hospital itself had a green and white color scheme.

The children's ward had three beds and a supply of Christmas toys for any child who might be unfortunate to find him or herself in the hospital over Christmas. The men's and women's ward each had eight beds in them and each ward opened into a separate sun parlor.

Miners' Hospital in Frostburg. Courtesy of the Albert and Angela Feldstein collection.

The kitchen, dining room, furnace room, drying room, ironing room and morgue could all be found on the ground floor. Also on the ground floor was the segregated ward for African-American patients.

It was a hospital that the coal towns in Allegany County were proud of. It could be seen in the fact that more than 3,000 people turned out to see the cornerstone laid for the hospital on Feb. 2, 1913.

A copper time capsule was also part of the cornerstone

ceremony. The report of Home Coming Centennial Committee; Souvenir Book of Frostburg; Home Coming invitation and badge; copies of the *Evening Times, Daily News, Press and American, Lonaconing Advocate, Baltimore American, Baltimore Sun;* statements of three banks; coins; bill for the General Assembly appropriation and a list of the hospital board of directors were all added to the time capsule.

Residents in the western edge of the county had waited a long time for their hospital. A bill had been introduced in 1908 for a Western Maryland hospital. "It was not pressed because of a contest between Midland and Frostburg for the hospital," the *Cumberland Evening Times* reported.

It was a debate that wasn't settled until Consolidated Coal Co. purchased two acres in Frostburg for the hospital. The hospital came about not only with the help of Consolidated Coal's donation, but the Maryland General Assembly contributed $25,000 toward the construction with the stipulation that the mining community be strongly represented on the board of directors. The board had to include a miner and a mine operator, in addition to two physicians and several town businessmen. Miner's Hospital was the first state-supported hospital in Maryland.

Dr. Helen A. Binnie of Wisconsin was hired as the hospital superintendent. She served until 1916 when she returned to Wisconsin to join her father's medical practice.

About eight months after the hospital opened, the *Cumberland Evening Times* noted another milestone for the hospital when Mrs. James Murphy of Grant Town, W.Va., was admitted.

"The arrival of a patient from another state at the Miner's Hospital is an indication that this institution, which has only been open for the reception of patients a little over a year, will at no distant day not be dependent on home patronage for support," the newspaper reported.

Miner's Hospital served as a hospital until the 1990s when it became St. Vincent de Paul Nursing Center. It is now called the Western Maryland Health System Frostburg Nursing and Rehabilitation Center.

Luke Gets Connected to Maryland

In the early 20th century, Luke was a thriving town with more than a thousand residents. It was home to one of the largest Allegany County employers. Despite this, you couldn't reach Luke from an Allegany County road, and even reaching the town on a Maryland road was a challenge.

"Westernport residents who wish to drive or walk to Luke, especially employees of the Luke paper mill, use the streets through Piedmont on the West Virginia side, crossing two bridges and two railroad crossings," the *Cumberland Evening Times* reported in 1938.

J. Glenn Beall was aware of this issue. He had started his political career as a member of the Allegany County Roads Commission. He served on the commission for seven years and became well aware of the road needs in the county. He left the commission when voters elected him to the Maryland State Senate.

As a member of the Maryland State Roads Commission, and he "decided to bring Luke, Md., back into the state in fact as well as in name," according to the *Cumberland Evening Times*. He not only believed that a road needed to connect Luke to the rest of Allegany County, but such a road would save commuters 10 minutes of drive time, reduce the heavy traffic on the Potomac River bridges, and improve safety for those commuters because the roads approaching the bridges had sharp curves that often led to accidents.

The commission approved a 4,000-foot-long new road along Franklin Hill from Washington Street in Westernport to Pratt Street in Luke in June 1938. The estimated construction time for the road would take 60 days.

While the Allegany County Commissioners were happy to see Luke connected to the county, they were concerned that the money for the road would reduce needed funded for other county road projects. Beall assured them in August that the money would come from the 1939 state reconstruction fund and wouldn't affect the county's regular roads funding. He also said the state would improve the road between Luke and Kitzmiller.

MD 135 was a less than 10 years, old and the bridge over the Savage River between Bloomington and Luke had been built the previous year.

In October, the Cumberland Contracting Company won a $159,239 for the relocating, grading, draining, and surfacing needed to build the new road.

"The big job was the Luke-Westernport Road, .91 mile long, the most outstanding from a construction standpoint of any road built in the Sixth District or perhaps in the State. The road was carved out of the mountain side just about the Western Maryland Railroad, and the only think making it possible was the nature of excavation, same being hard shale and rock, which fortunately occurred at points where any other type of material would have made job more expensive than it was," according to the *Report of the State Roads Commissioner of Maryland,* operating and financial report for fiscal year 1940.

The project also faced some rain delays and cost overruns with the final cost coming in at $213,117, according to the

Report of the State Roads Commissioner of Maryland. One additional benefit to the residents of Westernport was that because the construction caused such a bottleneck for traffic on Washington Street that the state built a new bridge over Georges Creek in town to help alleviate the traffic.

When the new road opened in 1940, people no longer had to travel outside of Maryland to reach Luke.

Get a Taste of Delicious Beef Ham

Beef ham was John Kinlock's dream come true. Literally. Born in Scotland in 1854, Kinlock was a 55-year-old butcher living on East Main Street in Lonaconing in 1909. It looked like it would be a good year for him.

The *Evening Times* credited him with inventing beef ham, based on a secret recipe that he had dreamed. It tasted great, and its popularity was growing. It looked like a new industry was coming to Lonaconing.

Although nearly everyone associates ham with pork, the work is not exclusive to swine. One definition of the word says that it is the meat at the back of the thigh or the thigh and buttock. So, beef ham means merely that the cuts of meat used are from the back of cow's or bull's thigh.

In 1909, the *Evening Times* reported, "The first foreign order for beef ham was received from New York last week and was promptly filled. It will soon become popular at Delmonico's and Sherry's, and the first thing you know there will be a big demand for Lonaconing beef ham and there will be a beef ham factory four stories high built on the island."

Kinlock had apparently sent a friend in New York beef ham and the fish dish, finnan haddie. It is cold-smoked haddock. It is a Scottish food that was smoked with green wood and peat.

Beef ham is also a Scottish dish. Kinlock apparently brought recipes for how to prepare it when he emigrated to America in 1875, but his beef ham was prepared it differently. Beef ham wherein in choice cuts of beef are prepared in spices. The difference seems to be the spices that Kinlock used and the cuts of beef. He prepared it differently enough that the *Evening Times* said that he had a patent on beef ham.

Beef ham was originated in Lonaconing in the early 1900s. Photo courtesy of Wikimedia Commons.

A chef at the Knickerbocker Club ate the beef ham and immediately wanted to serve it at the club. The Knickerbocker Club was a gentleman's club on 5th Avenue in New York that had been founded in 1871. It claimed many notable businessmen and politicians as members including President Franklin D. Roosevelt; H. Montagu Allan, banker and ship owner; Frank Crowninshield, developer of *Vanity Fair;* Congressman Robert Daniel; and banker and financier J. P. Morgan.

Plans were made to build a factory in Lonaconing to send Kinlock's beef ham all around the world.

"We'll supply the armies of the world, for beef ham needs no embalming or canning, the soldier can carry it in his blanket roll," the *Evening Times* reported.

Sadly, the expected explosion of people eating beef ham regularly never came to be. No notice can be found of the factory being built. However, beef ham is still available from Scottish butchers.

Kinlock died November 23, 1925, and was buried at the First Presbyterian Church cemetery.

The Allegany County Auto Industry

Allegany County's first venture into auto manufacturing was in an area known for paper, not cars.

Before the town of Luke and before the Mead-Westvaco paper mill, there was the Maryland Automobile Manufacturing Co.

Little is known about one of the pioneering car manufacturers in the country.

The factory is mentioned in the book published by Luke during its 50th anniversary in 1977. The book also reprinted an old newspaper article about a woman who was searching for information about the steam runabout.

Charles Lowndes, J. Phillip Roman, Howard Dickey, Albert Dumb and Brooke Whiting began the venture with $10,000 in capital stock. A Mr. Pagenhardt was the chief engineer.

The factory was located on the lower end of Luke on what is now Cromwell Street. It was set up in the former Pagenhardt Bicycle machine shops.

The Maryland Steamer, a steam roundabout, was built from 1900 to 1901 and sold all over the nation. The company's first delivery was in September 1900 when a racing car was sent to New York, according to Joe Weaver, former vice president of the Allegany County Museum. They also had five more orders for delivery vans. Other vehicles were sold to customers in Pittsburgh.

The vehicles used a vertical two-cylinder steam engine and chain drive. The bodies were made of wood and filled with large-diameter, wooden-spoke wheels with solid rubber tires, according to the book, *Maryland Automobile History*.

At the time of operation, there were only three other steam car manufacturers in the country. The company may have been ahead of its time or, perhaps, just poorly run. It went into receivership a year later because the owners couldn't pay their bills.

Nowadays, no one remembers the factory. There are still two photos in existence of the factory, but apparently, none of these classic autos still remains.

Cumberland's auto venture

There was a time when Motor City was going to be just that, a city of motors without the cars.

In 1918, cars were becoming more and more popular across the country. Automobile manufacturing was a growth industry, and many people were looking to become part of the manufacturing boom. Cumberland already had a piece of the pie with the Kelly-Springfield Tire Co. headquarters.

Then in April, the Paragon Motor Co. Board of Directors unanimously voted to change the proposed location of its plant from Connellsville, Pa., to Cumberland. The company opened offices in the J.P. Wiesel Building on Baltimore Street.

The board called Cumberland "one of the most-aggressive and wide-awake small cities in the United States" and "Cumberland, as an industrial center is, we find, admirably situated for the manufacture of Paragon Motor Cars..."

The site for the plant was twenty acres near the current

Motor City. The plan was to construct a $3 million plant that would employ 600 people and manufacture motors for the new line of cars. Paragon expected to produce about 500 cars a year.

That month, the *Cumberland Evening Times*, "Motor experts have pronounced the motor one of the most powerful and efficient in their knowledge."

Though Paragon intended to manufacture four cars, three prototypes were built. There was a two-passenger roadster, a two-passenger with a yacht deck (similar to a pickup truck) and a five-passenger sedan. They would sell for between $3,000 and $3,500, depending on the model. As Paragon officials toured potential building sites around the area, they drove the prototypes to advertise the future of motor cars.

Once the announcement was made, the company began selling stock to local residents who were excited to be part of the new venture. The one cautionary point was that although Paragon President Philip Blake was secretary of the Chamber of Commerce, the chamber withheld its support of the project. Because of his involvement with the company, Blake was asked to resign his position in June and did so.

In July, the chamber researched the idea and reported favorably on the mechanical design, construction, and performance of the Paragon cars. Executive Committee Chairman Henry Shriver wrote, "The Paragon Motor Car Co. has a very excellent car which will compare favorably with other well-known makes that have an established reputation throughout the country."

The problem was with the company's finances. The chamber noted that some information wasn't forthcoming and what was available suggested that Paragon would need to sell far too much stock to generate its needed working capital.

Despite the failure of the chamber to support the project,

the cornerstone was laid on Mount Savage Road on Aug. 28. The day's events began with a dance at 2:30 p.m. and the cornerstone ceremony at 4 p.m.

Cumberland Mayor Thomas Koon gave the opening remarks welcoming the beginning of a new industry in the area. Chamber President William Sperry poured the concrete for the first pier of the new building.

Thomas Pownell spoke at the ceremony. He said, "Our slogan is Build a Paragon here at Cumberland. ... Build one as good as the Ford and at Ford prices, and Henry Ford, the greatest motor man in all the world, will congratulate you, and the usefulness of the Paragon will be known from shore to shore."

He also said something that would become prophetic in how highly inaccurate it turned out to be, "I am glad, gentlemen, that booming and boasting (about the company) are absent, which omens that busting will be absent."

But a bust is actually what the entire project turned out to be.

In February and March of 1922, the chamber was running newspaper notices warning people about the dangers of fake stock-selling schemes.

In March, the chamber responded to a letter from Mrs. Wise, reminding her that the chamber hadn't endorsed the Paragon project. While she had not received her Paragon stock, the chamber told her there was little to be done except to contact the bank that issued the stock. The chamber also noted it had warned Paragon not to try and collect people who had backed out of stock purchases because the chamber would defend them.

Cumberland's chance to rival Detroit evaporated with crushed and costly dreams.

The French Sculptor From Lonaconing

To George Conlon, the egg was the pinnacle of evolution... at least regarding the shape of the human head.

"Don't laugh at the hen," Conlon said in a 1927 interview. "She has evolved from the egg; the American is evolving into one. Take a large egg in one hand and a mirror in the other. If you cannot readily distinguish between the two reflections, then you're 100 percent American; the ovoid ancestor of the 110 percent Americans with which the United States will, within the next few hundred years, be filled."

Conlon believed that because of the mix of cultures in America, American heads were becoming egg-shaped. He would be someone who would have known, too. In his day, Conlon, a native of Lonaconing, achieved fame in America and Europe for his sculptures of famous figures.

Among his subjects were Clarence Darrow, Charles Lindbergh, Blackjack Pershing, Amelia Earhart, and Will Rogers.

"A sculptor, you know, learns to read a man's character and possibilities from the shape of the skull," Conlon once said.

Conlon was born in Lonaconing to a working-class family. As a young man, he worked in the Georges Creek coal mines. It is there he began to discover his artistic talents.

"There the aspiring artist was reported to have made a bust of Maryland Governor Edwin Warfield from the plastic clay that was used to plug holes in the mine walls. Impressed by the portrait, the governor helped Conlon launch his art career," according to the U.S. Senate website.

Conlon attended the Maryland Institute College of Art in Baltimore and won the Rinehart Scholarship that allowed him to study at the Academie Julian and the Academie Colarossi in Paris.

This bust of Cordell Hull, former U.S. Secretary of State and "Father of the U.N.," is on permanent display in the U.S. Capitol. It was sculpted by Lonaconing native George Conlon and presented to Congress as a gift from the *Cumberland Evening Times* and Conlon in December 1944.

He married Mary Wilhowska in 1926, and they lived together in his Paris studio. The Nazis began their occupation of France in May 1940, and the Conlons obtained passports to return to America in June 1941. When George got the passports, he wife was visiting her sick mother in southern France. She remained with her mother planning to take a later ship to America. He lost contact with her after December 7, 1941, when the U.S. and France broke off communications. Mary Conlon died in June 1943 without ever seeing her husband again.

At the end of the war, Conlon sculpted a bust of Cordell Hull, former U.S. Secretary of State and "Father of the U.N." Conlon said he thought the shape of Hull's head made him an excellent subject for a sculpture.

Senator Millard Tydings of Maryland presented the bronze bust to Congress as a gift from the *Cumberland Evening Times* and Conlon. The bust is still on permanent display in the Capitol Building.

"In a joint resolution, adopted on December 4, 1944, Congress authorized the Joint Committee on the Library to accept the newspaper's gift. The bronze bust of Cordell Hull was unveiled in the Senate Reception Room the following year," according to the U.S. Senate website.

Conlon died in his sleep in his Washington D.C. home on December 14, 1980, at the age of 92.

Where is General Braddock's Lost Gold?

Somewhere between Cumberland, Md., and Pittsburgh, Pa., a chest of gold coins lies hidden with what could amount to a couple million dollars. It is buried beneath a tree at the confluence of two rivers according to the only survivor of the men who hid the chest from French soldiers and Indian warriors in 1755.

And yet, no one has found it.

The fact and the legend, obfuscated by more than 260 years, have led treasure hunters for years to wonder "Where is General Braddock's lost gold?"

Braddock's expedition

General Edward Braddock left Fort Cumberland on June 6, 1755, heading toward Fort Duquesne in Western Pennsylvania. The difficult terrain of steep mountain ridges and thick forests slowed their progress. Braddock's aide, George Washington, recommended splitting the army so that the best men could rush ahead and reach their destination while the rest of the army with the supplies would make its best time.

The gold was among the supplies. It was payroll money for the army. It would have also been used to pay Indians as guides and to keep them peaceful. Washington had brought it to Fort Cumberland from Williamsburg, Va., just before the army left.

When the army left Fort Cumberland is the last verifiable account of the gold.

A month later, the British were attacked by Indians working with the French. Around 500 soldiers were killed, another 500 wounded and just 300 survived without harm. Braddock was among the dead.

Only 28 Indians and Frenchmen were killed in the attack.

The gold was never seen again.

Indians working with the French attacked and killed General Braddock's men. The British troops were on their way to Fort Duquesne with a payroll chest but buried it before they were massacred. Photo courtesy of the Library of Congress.

Stories of burial

Legend says that before getting involved in the expected battle at Fort Duquesne, Braddock ordered the gold buried to keep it from the French. The plan was to recover it after the battle was won.

Braddock held a council among his officers and asked them

to wait until after the battle to get paid. They would not be able to spend the gold before then, and because casualties were expected in the fighting, there would be fewer men to divide the gold among after the battle.

The men agreed, and six soldiers transported the gold to a location at the confluence of two rivers and buried the chest under a walnut tree.

Shortly after that, Braddock was killed, and the remainder of the army retreated. No one ever returned to claim the gold.

Becoming legend

A story recounted in *Incredible, Strange, Unusual...* by Harold Scott recounts a story from May 1881. A Cumberland man driving along the National Road, which was built along Braddock's army route, was about 30 miles west of Cumberland when he saw an old man holding a crowbar.

The man stopped his horse to watch the old man. The old man said he was a descendant of one of the men who had buried Braddock's gold. The story passed down through his family was that the chest was buried where a large rock divided two streams. Members of his family had been trying to find the gold since Braddock's defeat.

In October 1941, rain washed Allegany County for three days. After it had ended, a hiker found a British coin on the road. The coin was close to a mountainside where water was still running off from the rainfall. Thinking the coin may have come from further up the mountain, the man began exploring and found another British coin. Though he searched for more on different occasions, the treasure eluded him.

Other rumors have appeared about the gold. In the 1950's, it was believed that the gold was buried where Crawford Run flows into the Youghiogheny River.

One story hypothesizes that the gold is still in Virginia in

Six soldiers buried a chest of gold before being massacred along with General Braddock's troops. The location of the treasure is now the stuff of legends. Photo courtesy of the Library of Congress.

Fairfax County. Charles Gilliss wrote about his theory in 1954 that because Braddock was having trouble moving his men and supplies through Virginia's wilderness, he left some things behind. Among the items were two, small brass cannons that had been filled with gold and capped with wooden plugs. Gilliss said the cannons were buried "two feet beneath the soil, fifty paces East of a spring, where the road runs North and South."

This account has been discredited, though, because Braddock and his army never came near the Centreville, Va.

Others believe that the French were able to recover the chest themselves and took it as spoils of war, though no one ever claimed credit for it.

Crewless Bomber Flies Over Allegany County

The 1,200-horsepower engines of the B-17 roared as it flew over Cumberland and then Ridgeley on the evening of November 21, 1943, but no one was on board the 27-ton bomber. The plane, which had flown 80 miles on its own, was losing altitude. It barely cleared slamming into Dan's Mountain, and around 7 p.m., it crashed near Midland.

"The bomber's crew of five men bailed out when engine trouble developed over the Alleghenies near Cherry Tree, Pa., eighty miles away, and all landed safely at least ten minutes before the craft, guided by its automatic pilot, finally pancaked on the knoll, two miles from Midland," the *Cumberland Evening Times* reported.

The B-17 was developed by Boeing in the 1930s and called the Flying Fortress. The planes were more than 74 feet long and had a wingspan of nearly 104 feet. They played a prominent role in the bombing of Germany during World War II.

The flight had been a routine trip to an air base in Dayton, Ohio, when the No. 4 engine developed problems. According to a 1999 article in *The Glades Star*, the pilot, Lt. Donald Crist, had the bomber flying in a large circular pattern at 7,000 feet for half an hour while he tried to restart the engine. Not only were his efforts unsuccessful, but ice started forming on the wings.

According to *The Glades Star*, Crist ordered the three enlisted men to bail out. He set the auto-pilot, and then he and his co-pilot parachuted out of the plane at 1,200 feet.

"The three enlisted men landed in a large field within walking distance of one another. The two officers who bailed out a minute or so later landed in a wooded area and their parachutes got caught in tree limbs," according to *The Glades Star*.

With the auto-pilot set, the plane flew another 80 miles before crashing into a mountain on Squirrel Hollow Road about two miles from Midland, just over the Garrett County line.

"The wings were sheared off by the terrific impact, and the motors were dislodged from the fuselage, but only the tail section was damaged by fire," the *Cumberland Evening Times* reported.

The Midland Volunteer Fire Department was quickly dispatched to put out any fires. Maryland State Troopers Joseph White and Ira Unger soon followed. They notified a local army recruiter, Tech. Sgt. Clarence Biehn, who notified the Army Air Force before heading out to the site.

By morning, internal security men from the Middletown, Pa., air base had the area cordoned off as they tried to salvage the wreck. Crist also showed up with one of his crewmen to search the wreckage for any personal effects.

Arthur Rees of Grantsville was a young boy at the time of the crash. He was interviewed for *The Glades Star* article and said that he and his friends tried to hike out to the crash site. "However, all we really got to see was where the tops of the trees had been broken off as it flew into the hillside. That was as close as we could get because there were guards there and no one was allowed to get any nearer."

He said that some people must have gotten in before the area was closed off and taken cockpit instruments as souvenirs. Authorities spent the next week asking people if they had the instruments or knew someone who did to turn them in.

While many people remember the B-52 bomber that crashed in Garrett County in 1964, this bomber crash has been largely forgotten.

County Veteran Who Survived Andersonville Prison Dies

When William Lowery died in Corriganville on April 30, 1923, most people thought the county had lost a friendly farmer. Yes, he was a Civil War veteran, but Lowery wasn't the first one to die, nor would he be the last one. However, he was a survivor of the most-notorious prison camp of the war.

Lowery enlisted as a 21-year-old in the 18th Pennsylvania Cavalry on October 29, 1862, when the regiment was organizing, and he served in Company K where he eventually was promoted to sergeant. He fought in skirmishes at Chantilly, Va., and the Battle of Gettysburg, among others.

During a Confederate attack on their regimental camp at Germania Ford, Va., Southern soldiers captured Lowery on November 18, 1863. He was held prisoner at Libby Prison and Danville Prison, both in Virginia, before he was sent to Andersonville, Ga.

The prison camp there was officially named Camp Sumter in honor of the county where it was located. Over the years, it has come to be known as Andersonville Prison Camp. It is also known for the poor conditions that existed there. It was overcrowded with four times as many prisoners as it was supposed to hold. The water supply and food rations were inadequate for the number of prisoners. The overcrowding also led to unsanitary conditions that allowed diseases like scurvy, diarrhea, and dysentery to run rampant.

The camp began at 16.5 acres but was enlarged to 26.5 acres. A 15-foot-tall wooden stockade wall enclosed the prison and ran around a 1,620 long and 779 wide area. "Approximately 19 feet inside of the stockade wall was the 'deadline,' which the prisoners were not allowed to cross. If a prisoner stepped over the 'deadline,' the guards in the 'pigeon roosts,' which were roughly thirty yards, apart were allowed to shoot them," according the National Park Service website for the camp.

A view of the poor living conditions in the overcrowded Andersonville Prison Camp in Georgia. Photo courtesy of Wikimedia Commons.

Lowery spent time in the prison hospital with "scorbutus" or scurvy. He was lucky. Scorbutus was listed as the cause of many deaths in Andersonville prison. He also survived the other challenges of the camp.

"He had been rarely ill during his 84 years, his worst physical ailment having been at Andersonville from lack of proper food. When he was released he was about dead and could barely raise his body on his hands and knees," the *Cumberland Evening Times* reported years later.

He was released from prison on April 6, 1865, and discharged from the army on June 19.

Of the 45,000 prisoners held at Andersonville during its 14 months in operation, nearly 13,000 of them died. Of the 17 members of Company K who were sent to Andersonville, only three men survived. Conditions at the camp were so bad that the camp commander, Capt. Henry Wirz, was executed for war crimes after the Civil War ended.

Following the war, Lowery returned to Allegany County. He worked for the Cumberland and Pennsylvania Railroad shops in Mount Savage. Despite his health issues, he was noted for his endurance and strength.

"He could lift with ease heavy objects which others could hardly budge," the newspaper reported.

Despite this, he filed a disability claim based on his time in the prison camp in 1879. It was settled three years later with him receiving $4 a month.

His family moved to Duquesne, Pa., at the turn of the century and lived there for 15 years before returning to Corriganville in 1917.

When he died in Allegany Hospital on April 30, 1923, he was survived by his wife of 54 years, Virginia, and five sons. However, his wife was bedbound with rheumatism and had been for seven years. She died a short time later.

His funeral was held in the family home in Corriganville. Charles W. Lanham, pastor of the Methodist Episcopal Church in Corriganville officiated. Lowery is buried in Greenmount Cemetery in Cumberland.

How a Small Town Got a State College

That Frostburg wants the Normal School,
 And Frostburg wants it badly,
But Cumberland, Oakland, and Hagerstown–
 They need it just as sadly.
This is stated with pleasure,
 Nor stated quite complete,
Because this rhyme is measured
 By a Frostburg maiden's feet.

- Daniel Webster Snyder
Cumberland Times

It was never a question whether Western Maryland wanted a normal school to train teachers. No, the fight was over where it would be located.

Through 1897, the Maryland Legislature talked about building a second normal school in the state. A normal school is a college where students train to be professional teachers, and Maryland's first normal school was in Baltimore.

On January 8, 1898, J. Benson Oder, editor of the *Frostburg Mining Journal*, wrote a letter in the newspaper to the county's legislative delegation proposing the second normal school be built in Frostburg. He pointed out that Frostburg had the best water and sanitation in the region, and Cumberland had already received more than its fair share of "county favors."

"Gentlemen, once again, *you owe this debt to your constituents. Pay it* and thus erect a monument to your legislative memory that will outlast all the mine inspectorships that you can lay at the feet of Piney Ridge," Oder wrote.

J. Benson Oder

A normal school was also expected to improve education in the county without having to send prospective teachers to Baltimore for schooling. Betty Van Newkirk wrote in the *Journal of the Alleghenies* that in 1880, all but three of the teachers in Allegany County were certified, but 121 of the

124 teachers had had to do it without normal school training.

The idea of a Western Maryland normal school caught on, and Hagerstown and Oakland soon threw their hats in the ring as a location for the school. However, in Western Maryland, Cumberland was the 400-pound gorilla in the room.

"Cumberland has no quarrel with its neighbors and is seeking none," the *Cumberland News* reported. "Its people would welcome within its limits the location of such an institution as is proposed. It is so situated geographically, has such ample railway and other facilities as would suggest this to be the nature point for the school."

This upset Oder, who believed that Cumberland already had enough largesse from the state.

"That if the Normal School is to be located at Frostburg, the most suitable in the county, Cumberland influence will smash the Normal School!

"Why Cumberland, conjoined with ministerial officiousness, keeps us out of even one Sunday train, and then makes success in matters like that an argument against us by citing its only superior 'railway facilities,'" Oder wrote.

Meanwhile, Cumberland sent a delegation to Annapolis to lobby the legislative delegation. Cumberland's plan was to have the state build a $25,000 dormitory next to the Allegany Academy (the present Washington Street public library) and then support the school with $5,000 a year to cover expenses.

Frostburg responded by forming its own committee to come up with a proposal.

Then, in late January 1898, the Allegany County Teachers' Institute met in Cumberland and voiced its support for having the normal school in that city.

"The adoption of a resolution by the Teachers' Institute at Cumberland naming that city as the proper place for the Normal School should have no weight on determining the location of the school," Oder wrote in the *Mining Journal*. "By what right the teachers, the employes of the people, should attempt to dictate the location of any school is not known. This is a matter for the people who pay the taxes to decide. The teachers are the employes of the taxpayers and should remain silent on the subject."

The fight over where to locate the proposed school raged as the time for legislative session to end drew closer.

Cumberland, Oakland, or Frostburg?

In 1898, the Maryland Legislature was in agreement that a second normal school for the training of teachers should be built, and it should be built in Western Maryland.

It made sense. The first normal school had been built in Baltimore, the largest city in the state. Perhaps, Normal School No. 2 should be built in the second-largest city in Maryland. Cumberland officials certainly wanted the legislature to think like that.

Frostburg officials disagreed. The *Frostburg Mining Journal* had first proposed building the normal school in Western Maryland, but Editor J. Benson Oder had promoted building it in Frostburg.

The *Lonaconing Star* reported, "The logical place for its location is at Frostburg, and we hope it will be built there. We are assured that Cumberland will not oppose the measure on account of the location of the school, yet we feel that there is a disposition somewhere to have it in Cumberland or not build it all."

Sen. David Dick introduced a bill in the legislature to have the school built in Cumberland on Feb. 9, saying it was "the logical place."

Oder wrote, "Cumberland is also 'the logical place' for typhoid fever and all other bacterial diseases," referring to the poor sanitation in the city.

Another bill was introduced on Feb. 24, siting the school in Frostburg. Then a bill was introduced in the Maryland Senate on Mar. 22 to locate the school in Oakland.

Oder commented on the latter, saying, "Oakland is better than Cumberland. But there are hundreds of acres of gladeland malaria around Oakland."

The argument soon became locate the school in Cumberland or don't build it, just as Oder had predicted.

In March, the *Cumberland News*, thinking that Cumberland would be the location of the school, attempted to be conciliatory. "It is hoped to be hoped that the paper does not truly reflect the opinion of the citizens of that town which ought to show a spirit of fraternity towards its neighbors."

Oder pointed out that Cumberland showed no fraternity towards Frostburg when the state fireman's convention was planned there. Hotels in Cumberland ran ads saying Frostburg had no accommodations, which cost Frostburg hotels money. The Cumberland Academy of Music also refused to book any act that also planned on playing in Frostburg.

Finally, on Apr. 2, the *Mining Journal* announced that the bill approving $20,000 to build the normal school in Frostburg passed. Being truly conciliatory, the *Cumberland News* reported, "While Cumberland made an effort to have the school erected here, Frostburg out-generated her and carried off the prize. Frostburg people are hustlers and when they start after anything they usually accomplish their mission."

Then on April 16, Gov. Lloyd Lowndes, wrote a Frostburg resident, saying, "Replying to your favor of April 7, it gives me pleasure to say that the bill containing the appropriation for a State Normal School at Frostburg has been duly signed and is now a law."

Maryland Normal School No. 2 would be built in Frostburg.

James Rada, Jr.

Lloyd Lowndes, Jr.

It took behind-the-scenes workings to get a college in Frostburg

Gov. Lloyd Lowndes' announcement that Frostburg would get Normal School No. 2 to train teachers brought joy to the people in Frostburg who had fought hard to have the school in their town. However, it also brought confusion to anyone who had followed the progress of Maryland Legislature.

Legislators had introduced bills to locate the normal school in Cumberland, Frostburg, and Oakland. Although the Frostburg bill made it the furthest through the process, the Senate Committee on Finance gave it an unfavorable review on April 4, 1898, and it ended there.

At this point, many people believed not only wouldn't Frostburg get a normal school, the state wouldn't build a second one.

However, much was going on behind the scenes. "On March 31, when even the bill's strongest proponents admitted defeat, Captain T. F. McCardell, one of the Comptroller's department, who had ties of blood and friendship with Frostburg, met with Senator [David] Dick and Delegates [James] Campbell, [Matthew] Rowe, and [John] Leake," Betty Van Newkirk wrote in the *Journal of the Alleghenies*.

McCardell wanted Leake to submit an amendment allocating the money for a normal school in Frostburg to the general appropriations bill when it came up for a vote. He also got the delegations of Somerset, Baltimore, Frederick, Harford, and Carroll counties and some of the Baltimore City delegation to agree to the language of the amendment. The amendment set aside $20,000 for the construction of a normal school in Frostburg and $5,000 annually for its operation on the condition the people of Frostburg deeded a suitable piece of property to the state for the school.

Although this seems the likely version of events, Del. Campbell told people he inserted the amendment into the bill.

"'Uncle Jimmie' as he was familiarly known to his many friends, often told how he, having access to the Budget Bill, inserted the amendment creating the school after the Appropriation Bill had been completed by the Ways and Means Committee," John L. Dunkle, former principal/president of Normal School No. 2/Frostburg State Teachers College from 1923 to 1945 wrote in an article in *Tableland Trails*.

The latter story would explain why Sen. Dick expressed reservations about the legality of the amendment, although the amendment had other problems that might have concerned him. It didn't express who would receive the sums of money being promised, and its enactment hinged on the people of Frostburg finding a suitable site for the school.

The legislative record seems to support the former, though, showing that Leake proposed the amendment, and the legislature supported it.

"It seems highly probable that the amendment was accepted by the House of Delegates only to quiet the Allegany County delegation and get on with other business; nothing was expected to come from it," Newkirk wrote.

Even after its passage, many legislatures thought Gov. Lowndes would strike it out because the money wasn't available.

However, after the state's attorney deemed the amendment legal, Lowndes signed the bill with the amendment in it.

Now, the pressure fell on Frostburg residents to find a suitable site.

Picking the perfect land for a school

Getting Maryland to build Normal School No. 2 in Frostburg in 1898 was a victory for the town, but the work to get the school open and running was just beginning.

When the legislature finally passed the bill and Governor Lloyd Lowndes signed it, $20,000 had been allocated to build the school to train teachers, and $5,000 a year had been allocated to support the school's operation "provided that the people of the town of Frostburg furnish the ground for the site of said building and deed the same to the state."

School commissioners John G. Wilson and H. G. Weimer visited Frostburg in May to meet with a committee Mayor Joseph Bear appointed to find the site for the school. They discussed what the site needed and potential places in town that met those qualifications.

Meanwhile, the Maryland attorney general weighed in on what to do about the fact that the legislation the governor signed didn't state who was in charge of the school funds. The attorney general decided that the Maryland State Board of Education would handle the money and "that opinion is in exact accord with the design of the framers and projectors of the proposition and with the wished of the people of Frostburg," the *Frostburg Mining Journal* reported.

The Town of Frostburg advertised for properties and their purchase prices in July 1898, which ignited a new fight in town over where the normal school should be built.

"The Journal would rather have it at Sand Spring or Borden Mine than not have it at all, but what is the use to bury it in some out-of-the-way place?" the *Mining Journal* reported.

Rev. Alexander C. Haverstick was appointed the chairman of the committee to raise the funds to purchase the property for the school. His committee members started going door to door in the region and encountered some reluctance.

J. Benson Oder, editor of the *Mining Journal*, said, "A body of people who can afford to pay without apparent kicking $2,800 a year for light and get back nothing but light ought not to hesitate an instant to subscribe $2,000..." He pointed out that for that investment, the school was expected to bring $15,000 to $30,000 a year to the region.

This may have helped because by the time the governor and members of the state board of education arrived in Frostburg on Aug. 6, the town had $2,000 committed from residents.

Newly elected Mayor C. F. Nickel, former mayor Joseph Bear, Haverstick, F. C. Beall, Dr. T. Griffith, Hon. James Dando, and Oder met the state group at the train station and escorted the state delegation to the Gladstone Hotel.

The board held a special session at the hotel and opened the 13 property bids. The Frostburg group then escorted the governor and board around town to all the sites.

The *Cumberland News* noted, "Every location was visited and no attempt was made to influence the board in the selection of any one site."

The group returned to the hotel to eat dinner and then went to Mount Savage to visit with Capt. John Sheridan.

Around 10 p.m., Lowndes called Haverstick and told him the board had selected the Beall's Park site. The *Mining Journal* noted that the owners of the chosen site hadn't planned to offer it as an option, but it was "a site perhaps not as eligible as some, but better than others. The park was not offered by F. C. Beall, executor, but someone inveigled him into naming his price, $2,000, and, against his protest, it was considered by the Board, with the result stated."

The original three-acre lot for the normal school was on a slight decline with lots of massive oak trees on it.

Oder wrote in the *Mining Journal* that the site wasn't ideal in one respect, but he doesn't mention what that is.

Betty Van Newkirk wrote in *Journal of the Alleghenies*, "In retrospect, it seems probably the defect loomed even larger in the minds of the Governor and his committee, and that they deliberately chose the Park in a last effort to thwart the town's hopes for a normal school."

She suspected that the defect in the site was that it sat as a buffer zone between the white and black communities in Frostburg.

"[Gov. Lowndes] must have felt confident that, in the unlikely event that the Beall family would agree to sell the land, the citizens would find a school for their children in that location absolutely unthinkable," Newkirk wrote.

That wasn't the case.

The fundraising committee then began collecting all the hundreds of pledges residents had made. Some contributors included the Frostburg Bicycle Club ($65) and the Ancient Order of Hibernians ($50). C. K. Lord, with Consolidation Coal Company and the Cumberland and Pennsylvania Railroad, pledged $100 from each company. Hundreds of individual donations came in for as little as 25 cents. This might sound small, but this came from miners, who, in some cases, earned $5 a week, once all the deductions were made from their pay.

The fundraising committee reached the $2,000 goal and surpassed it in two weeks. An excess of $114.87 was later returned to the city's coffers because all the town's $250 pledge was not needed.

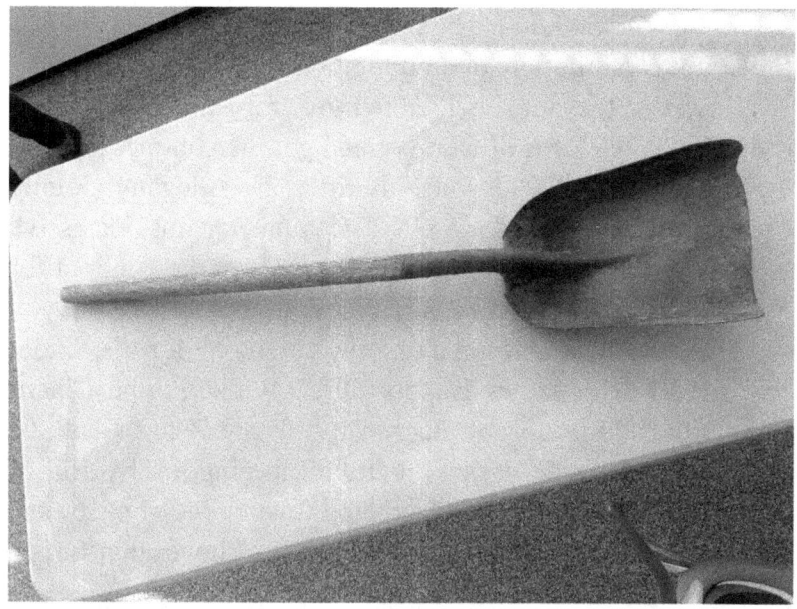

The shovel used for the groundbreaking of Maryland Normal School No. 2. Photo courtesy of the Frostburg Museum.

The college opens

With a site chosen for a new normal school in Frostburg in 1898, Alfred Mason, the architect chosen for the project, went to work. In March 1899, he announced he expected work on the project to begin in April. His building designs showed a three-story building with eight classrooms, a large assembly hall, principal's office, teachers' offices, and a modern laboratory for science classes.

However, when the bids for the building were opened in May, all of them significantly exceeded the $20,000 the State of Maryland allocated for the project. This meant Mason had to scale back his project, which delayed the projected opening for the school.

The bids for the revised project were opened in June, and although they were much closer to the budget, they were all still more than $20,000. The bids also didn't include the costs for heating, ventilation, and plumbing the building.

However, the state decided to move forward with the project. Martens & Sons of Cumberland got the contract to build the school for $21,000, but only after the Allegany County Commissioners offered a $5,000 guarantee against excessive costs. Weaver and Hoffman of Baltimore got the contract for heating, ventilation, and plumbing for $2,753.

The town held a groundbreaking ceremony for the school on June 27 with James Dando, C. H. Walker, John Chambers, Otto Hohing, Joseph Baer, C. O. Towles, F. C. Beall, G. G. Townsend, and J. Benson Oder all turning a shovelful of dirt. Chambers was so proud of the town's accomplishment at getting the school that he displayed the shovel that turned the first dirt in his store window afterwards.

The cornerstone laying event was held on September 1, 1899. Schoolchildren gathered at Beall High School and walked with teachers to event.

Officials met at the Gladstone Hotel and formed a procession from there. Led by the Quaker City Band; state, county, and local officials; members of the local and state Masonic Lodges; and citizens marched down Broadway to Loo Street where 2,500 people gathered at the building site.

Items of the day were placed in the cornerstone before it was sealed. These included: a copy of the last annual report from the Grand Lodge of Maryland A.F. and A. M., a copy of Masonic Ritual of Laying the Cornerstone, a copy of the *Frostburg Mining Journal* that listed the contributors to the fund used to the purchase the land for the school, the latest copies of the three Frostburg newspapers, coins from 1899, and a Grand Army of the Republic badge John Dennison contributed.

Frostburg Mayor C. F. Nickel told the gathering, "Shortly on this foundation of native rock, therefore, will be erected a building within whose walls will be taught both the theoretical and practical lessons of life whose influence for good will be felt long after this generation has joined the silent majority."

He also lightly touched on the controversy surrounding locating the normal school in Frostburg.

"In locating the school here no mistake has been made," Nickel said. "But there will be views expressed, no doubt, by speakers here today of the advantages accruing to Frostburg, but we believe the exchange of benefits will be an even one. Who will say Frostburg is not the ideal spot for this school-with our grand mountain scenery, pure air, fresh sandstone water, our stalwart, order-loving men and charming women, and situated at the culminating end of this great valley, populous with an industrious, intelligent, appreciative people? Where could have been found a more picturesque, healthy, deserving environment?"

Governor Lloyd Lowndes was also on hand to congratulate the people of Frostburg on their efforts to bring the normal school to their town.

Although the cornerstone was laid in 1899, the efforts to complete the building and open the school were not over.

Betty Van Newkirk wrote in a *Journal of the Alleghenies* article that it was obvious by January more money would be needed to complete the school and it wouldn't be coming from the state. The county used its guarantee to keep the project moving, but it expected the money back. It wasn't until $15,000 was included in a 1902 omnibus bill that the school could be completed.

The college opened on September 15, 1902, with 57 students attending, and it has been growing ever since.

A Bridge Over Troubled Waters

So close, and yet so far away.
That's what many Oldtown residents must have thought when the railroad tie plant opened in Green Spring, W. Va., in 1911. Sure, the plant and the jobs it offered were only a few miles away, but to reach it from Maryland, residents had to cross the Potomac River. That meant they would either have long waits to cross the river on a ferry or drive 14 miles to Cumberland, cross a bridge over the river, and drive back to Green Spring. Then repeat the route to get back to Oldtown.

Melvin R. Carpenter lived in Hancock, but he worked as a tie inspector in Green Spring. He crossed the river multiple times each day as traveled to Cumberland to conduct business. He would use the ferry to cross the river unless high water halted operations, which was more than a few times a year. Even when the ferry operated, the long wait to cross the river was frustrating.

He came up with an idea to build a bridge across the river in the early1920s. The dream may have seemed quite simple, but the execution was something altogether different.

"The bridge was plagued with land disputes, government red tape, a lengthy drawn out charter. There were entitlement arguments over property rights, dozen or more permits and even an act of Congress before the first toll could be collected in the fall of 1938," Green Spring resident Belinda Sue wrote about the bridge.

Carpenter formed the Green Spring Oldtown Bridge Company and sold shares in the company to raise funds to build the bridge and many of the early supporters were employees of the tie plant who wanted a quicker way to work. They also planned the bridge they wanted to build.

One of the early problems the company ran into was that property owners along the river demanded high prices for the needed parcels. This led to drawn-out negotiations that lasted years. Some cases even required legal proceedings to condemn the property because the owner was trying to price gouge.

Trying to secure government permits in two states also brought the plans for a bridge to a standstill. Besides having to deal with state and local governments, it also took an act of Congress to build the bridge. In August 1935, the U.S. Congress passed legislation allowing Carpenter to sink large concrete pillars into the riverbed to support the bridge and use it for public use. The U.S. War Department also had to approve modified plans for the bridge after the 1936 St. Patrick's Day flood, according to newspaper reports.

Each step forward was another victory in a project that took nearly two decades to complete. Carpenter and his supporters persevered because the communities needed the bridge.

Local labor, some of them loaned to the project by the tie plant, worked 10 hours days, earning 25 cents an hour, building the bridge.

"We drilled deep holes in solid rock and stuck angle iron in the holes," said Robert Koontz, one of the workers, in 1996. "Then we poured a 16-inch footer so that the irons stuck up out of it and pointed upstream. We made cement from sand and gravel in the river and poured the piers out of that."

The bridge deck was nailed to 4x6-inch hardwoods with railroad rails beneath that.

"I wouldn't be afraid to drive a locomotive over it," Koontz told the *Cumberland Times-News*.

The low-water bridge finally opened on December 13, 1938, when the last of three temporary bridges that had been used in the preceding months were removed. The final bridge offered minimal resistance to floodwaters and was expected to be open 98 percent of the year, according to the *Cumberland Evening Times*.

"He built his bridge just high enough for water to pass under it after ordinary rains. It is low enough for ice to flow over it when the river is high," the newspaper reported.

The toll was 25 cents for each vehicle and 10 cents for bikes and walkers.

"At least thirty miles will be saved by people making a round trip between Cumberland and Green Spring area," the *Cumberland Evening Times* reported.

Commutes that had taken close to an hour now took only minutes.

Because Maryland owned the Potomac River along its southern border, the Maryland legislature claimed control over the bridge operation, although it hadn't wanted to help with funding its construction. This was upsetting to locals involved in the project since the company had been chartered in West Virginia and fund raised primarily in Hampshire County. Much of the manpower to build the bridge and materials also came from Green Spring.

Despite the bad feelings, an agreement was reached to keep the bridge operating privately.

Carpenter sold the bridge in 1970. By this time, more than 2.5 million crossings had been made on it. It has gone through a few owners since, but it continues to offer residents a convenient way to travel between Oldtown and Green Spring. It also happens to be the only private bridge in the U.S. involved in interstate travel.

Acknowledgements

I wanted to thank all of those people who helped me put the *Secrets of Allegany County* together. The longer I work as a writer, the more I realize that while one person may publish a book, the effort is much richer when others assist.

I've been writing articles about the history of Allegany County for decades. I've been doing the Secrets books for five years. I'm surprised it took me so long to get around to doing *Secrets of Allegany County*.

One great local resource over the years for Western Maryland history is the Western Maryland Historical Library (whilbr.org). It has tons of information and pictures about historical topics in Washington, Allegany, and Garrett counties. Anyone interested in the history of the area should have it bookmarked on their computer.

I'd also like to thank Jan Alderton, former editor for the *Cumberland Times-News* and Al Feldstein. You may have noticed that many of the pictures in the book come from Al's collection, but he has also been a source of information when I have questions about a place and person in the county's history. Jan is the person who started me writing about the history of the county when I was a reporter at the newspaper.

Finally, I'd like to thank Grace Eyler for not only another great-looking cover but also being able to create the template for the Secrets series.

JAMES RADA, JR.

I have probably missed someone who I'll remember after this book goes to print. If so, it's not because I didn't appreciate your input. I sometimes get confused juggling all of the projects that I do. If I did leave you out, mention it to me.

Meanwhile, I'm off to work on my next project.

James Rada, Jr.
January 1, 2022

About the Author

James Rada, Jr. is an Amazon.com bestselling author of historical fiction and non-fiction history. They include the popular books *Strike the Fuse, Canawlers,* and *Battlefield Angels: The Daughters of Charity Work as Civil War Nurses.*

He lives in Gettysburg, Pa., where he works as a freelance writer. James has received numerous awards from the Maryland-Delaware-DC Press Association, Associated Press, Maryland State Teachers Association, Society of Professional Journalists, and Community Newspapers Holdings, Inc. for his newspaper writing.

If you would like to be kept up to date on new books being published by James or ask him questions, he can be reached by e-mail at *jimrada@yahoo.com.*

To see James' other books or to order copies on-line, go to *www.jamesrada.com.*

PLEASE LEAVE A REVIEW

If you enjoyed this book, please help other readers find it. Reviews help the author get more exposure for his books. Please take a few minutes to review this book at *Amazon.com* or *Goodreads.com*. Thank you, and if you sign up for my mailing list at *jamesrada.com*, you can get FREE ebooks.

WANT TO KNOW MORE SECRETS?

Find out the little-known stories and hidden history of Maryland and Pennsylvania with the Secrets series from James Rada, Jr.

Available wherever books are sold.

www.ingramcontent.com/pod-product-compliance
Lightning Source LLC
Chambersburg PA
CBHW072004070526
44583CB00015B/1333